LIES AT HER DOOR

by A.A. Abbott

LARGE PRINT EDITION

Edited by Katharine D'Souza Editorial Services.

Proofreading by PG Print & Office Services.

Cover design by Getcovers.

Published by Perfect City Press.

This book was written by a British writer in British English. Dialect terms like 'my lover' are occasionally used.

ISBN 978-1-913395-09-4

A FEW WORDS OF THANKS

Thanks to my editor, Katharine D'Souza, and everyone else who helped make this book great, especially Ali AElsey, Andrea Neal, Colin Butcher, David Wake, David Ward, Dawn Abigail, Dennis Zaslona, Donna Finn, Donna Morfett, Elizabeth Hill, Helen Combe, Jeremy White, Jo Ullah, Kevin Carter, Margaret Egrot, Marie Wright, Michèle Weibel, Nicki Collins, Nigel Howl, Paula Good, Prudence S Thomas, René Gapert, Samantha Cross, Steve Pelzer, Steven Keogh, Suzanne H Ferris, Suzanne McConaghy, Tom Blenkinsop, Tracey Preater and Verity Dadd.

A.A. Abbott
England, June 2022

Contents

JULY 2000

CHAPTER 1

NEIL

The music rose from the earth. He was alone in this massive garden, yet somehow a melody surrounded him. The four-year-old boy darted around the lawn, failing to find headphones or speakers. He peeked at the hedge that enclosed the plot, the black-railed gate that broke the ring of glossy green leaves, and the five trees at the edges. Earlier, he'd counted them and been proud of himself. Now, hearing the sound was louder beneath it, he drew closer to the largest. Frilly-edged leaves tickled his cheek. He began to dance.

The rhythm was fast. Shrieking with delight, he twirled round and round. As he expected, giddiness overcame him and he fell to the ground, laughing. Lying on the warm, yellowed grass, he could feel a drumbeat pulsing through it. Who was playing the tune? Did fairies live in the tree? He hummed along with them.

The music stopped.

The boy stared up at the tree's canopy looming above, then down at its solid trunk. All was still. The world was quiet again, and it had finished spinning.

He staggered to his feet. His elation had subsided and he wanted his mother. He fumbled with the latch of the gate. When it opened, he bolted onto the cobbled path that ran between the hedge and a row of houses. They were tall and white. One had a red door. In the front yard outside it, he had left his mother talking to her new friend.

"Mummy!" He chuckled with relief as he saw the two women sitting together, sipping tea and smoking. His mother waved.

He hurtled into her, clutching at her trousers. "Mummy, there are fairies in the garden. I heard them singing."

"Don't be silly, Neil." She flicked ash from her cigarette. It landed in one of the pots of pink flowers near her feet. Today, she wore shiny black shoes. They glinted in the sunlight. For hours, she had stood in those shoes, talking to strangers in a huge room crammed with tables, chairs, and chatty people. Neil had been on his best behaviour, sitting quietly with small toys he'd been given. There was a squeezy ball, a little puzzle, and some pencils. He had been good; playing in the garden was his reward.

His mother's friend, the lady called Jennifer, smiled at him with scarlet lips. "You're bored, aren't you, Neil? I'll get my daughter to come and amuse you. She's thirteen and she loves children."

He flinched as Jennifer's bony fingers reached towards him. When lacquered nails ruffled his hair, he willed himself to stand still.

"He's a cutie," Jennifer said. "I bet Lucy would babysit for you. Why not leave him here tonight, and you can come to the conference dinner with me? Bristol University's catering isn't bad. Anyway, we both know all the business is done in the bar at these events."

His mother said, "Isn't thirteen a bit young?"

"She'd be thrilled," Jennifer said. "It does her good to take on adult responsibilities. Stops her getting spoilt. She won't be by herself, either. My son will be around to keep an eye on them. He's in his twenties."

Neil could barely count to thirteen. He imagined anyone of that age must be grown up. Twenty was beyond him.

His mother was silent, which Jennifer took as agreement.

"Great," Jennifer said. "I'll introduce Lucy, then we can sort out the paperwork for your book order. I'm glad I can help." She stood and stretched, calling for her daughter as she vanished behind the red door.

Neil couldn't pretend to understand. He held out his arms for his mother to pick him up. She dandled him on her knee, her dark trousers stark against the white metal chair, ornate like lace. A matching table held an ashtray, teapot, cups, and a plate of shortbread. There was a notepad too, in which she had been writing. Her fingers were inky. An unfamiliar smell of tobacco clung to her. He knew people smoked sometimes, but he didn't remember her doing it before. This was no ordinary day, though. She had taken Neil to work, and then to Jennifer's house, and accepted Jennifer's offer of 'just one, to keep me company'.

"You heard," his mother said. "Jennifer thinks Lucy should babysit for you later. Would you like that?"

He wasn't sure what she meant, but he knew what he would really like. His mouth watered as he gazed at the shortbread.

His mother's eyes followed his. Laughing, she handed him a piece.

Jennifer reappeared, trailed by another female nearly as tall and much wider.

"This is Lucy," Jennifer said. "Why don't you play with Neil in the garden, Lucy? Mrs Slater and I have business to discuss."

"Hello." Lucy smiled. Her messy hair, the colour of rope, swung over her face as she reached down for the plate.

Jennifer placed her hand over her daughter's. "They're not for you, Lucy."

"Sorry." Lucy's smile dimmed, glowing again as she turned to Neil. Her blue eyes twinkled. "Let's play in the garden. Mum said you were frightened, but you needn't be. There's nothing scary here. Cross my heart and hope to die."

DECEMBER 2019

CHAPTER 2

LUCY

Handsome and monied, the houses of Jackson Crescent slotted neatly into Bristol's upmarket Clifton district. A snow-white terrace, front yards behind railings, swept in a curve off Jackson Road and then joined it again. A straight row of similar properties backed onto Jackson Road. The focal point of the crescent was the communal garden in its centre, a semi-circle planted with grass and trees. Already, fairy lights would be strung up, the hedge clipped and fallen leaves tidied away. The space would be perfect for the residents' carols that night, when wealth and success would be on display, all darkness buried deep in the past.

Lucy Freeman couldn't see the garden from the rear of number 13, but she still tingled with anticipation. Like fantasy novels and online games, music was a means of escape. Without it, she was just a chubby loser living with her parents at the age of thirty-two.

"Alexa, play madrigals," she instructed.

The virtual assistant obliged, sending the strains of 'Come Away Sweet Love' through her second-floor bedroom. Lucy joined in with the soprano part. A warm glow spread through her as she remembered childhood days singing with her brother and mother. In those rare moments, she'd experienced a sense of belonging and approval. Now Daniel was coming home for Christmas. With luck, he'd arrive in time for carols with the neighbours.

Would it be the same as the old days? She'd be kidding herself if she fancied his rock star lifestyle had splintered off her brother from the rest of the family. He'd become distant well before then, after his best friend disappeared in France. According to her mother, it had been Lucy's fault and shouldn't be discussed further.

Daniel had made it clear he didn't wish to talk about it either. As the years passed, she'd never raised the subject with him. The space between them grew wider as he joined a glitzy world she could only dream about. While they weren't close, she'd enjoy seeing him. The neighbours would be ecstatic, of course. A rock icon's presence lent glamour to the evening and fuel to their gossip.

A dog barked. Lucy peered outside at number 13's back garden and busy Jackson Road beyond. There was no sign of an animal. A recycling lorry clattered past, its tins and bottles rattling. She raised her voice, then stood on tiptoe to stare through the other window in her room. This was on the end wall, a tiny porthole giving a bird's-eye view of Brian and Marilyn's place on the opposite corner.

Lucy's father was rapping on the smart brass doorknocker. From above, she saw a bald patch amid his neat grey hair. Sebastian looked every inch the academic, tall and stooped, a smart charcoal jacket almost hanging off his thin figure. Her mother, Jennifer, was elegant in a spangled shawl. Lucy squinted, unable to make out Jennifer's red lips and smoky eyeshadow, but still proud of them. She liked working on Jennifer's cosmetics for her, even though she never used them herself. There wasn't much point. 'Why put lipstick on a pig?' as Jennifer had once said.

Her parents allowed chatty Marilyn to air-kiss them, then Sebastian pushed Jennifer's wheelchair inside. The invitation for afternoon drinks had been addressed to Sebastian, Jennifer and Lucy, but Brian had told her she wasn't expected if it suited her to stay away. He supposed she didn't have much time to herself, he'd said, as Lucy nodded gratefully. Perhaps he understood how she dreaded polite conversation with a bunch of people twice her age.

Finally alone, Lucy's gaze flitted to her laptop. Switched off and forlorn, it called to her. She wished she could wield a magic talisman, defeat dragons and loot temples online just for an hour. Perhaps there would be time later when she'd finished her tasks for Christmas Eve. There was so much to do: presents to wrap and food to prepare for the big day.

A series of louder barks interrupted her thoughts.

"Alexa, stop."

Lucy glanced out of the rear window again. To her astonishment, a fluffy white dog capered across the back garden. This was a small square of lawn bounded by the house, a garage opposite giving out onto Jackson Road, and high stone walls on either side. There was no obvious way in. Lucy rubbed her eyes. When she removed her hands, the dog remained in sight. It was yelping at a high pitch now, frantically scrabbling at a wall.

Concerned about the creature's distress, Lucy ran down three flights of stairs. She rested, breathless, against the French doors in the basement kitchen. Outside in the garden, the dog noticed her. It pressed its nose to the glass, whining and wagging its bushy tail. Enveloped in a cloud of snowy fur, it was a handsome animal and appeared well cared for.

"We'd better find out who you belong to, boy," Lucy murmured, feeling foolish at speaking to a dog and uncertain it would understand. Presumably, it would have an owner's tag on its collar. Could it be bribed with biscuits to let her check? She shook a few crackers from a tin she'd planned to serve with cheese on Christmas Day.

Snacks in hand, she opened the door. Accompanied by a gust of wind, the dog leaped inside, nearly bowling Lucy over. It stopped, sniffed at her fingers, and whimpered.

"Here boy." Having closed the door, she offered the crackers. They vanished in seconds. A hot, wet tongue licked every crumb off her hand.

"Let's see if there's a clue." She knelt down. The dog seemed friendly enough, but would it bite? Tentatively, Lucy reached for the collar.

Still amiable, the animal stood still. Lucy found a brass disc with a mobile number. Retrieving her phone from a pocket, she typed in the digits.

"Who's that?" At the sound of the man's voice, the dog's ears pricked up.

"I'm Lucy Freeman. Er, I've got your dog. Will you come and collect it?"

"Depends where you are. Bristol, I presume?"

"Yes, Jackson Crescent."

"Then no. I'm out of the country. My mother's looking after Sasha for me. Do you know Margaret Forsyth at number 12?"

"That's next door."

It began to make sense. Margaret, Lucy's occasional employer, owned a garden flat. Lucy supposed Sasha had either climbed over the adjoining wall or tunnelled under it.

"Want me to call her?" Margaret's son asked.

"No, I'll do it. I've got her number." Lucy already felt guilty about disturbing him. He must be with other people, perhaps at a business meeting; there was a babble of conversation in the background.

It wasn't long before Margaret stood at the front door, stylish in a purple cape trimmed with black velvet and fulsome in her apologies.

"I am so terribly sorry. I don't know why I agreed to take this dog." Her brown eyes nevertheless sparkled with amusement. She handed Lucy a box of Cadbury's Milk Tray. "Can you use a few more chocolates, do you think?"

"Thank you." She would offer them round when Daniel arrived. "I like your eyeshadow, by the way."

It was a shimmery gold, perfectly suited to Margaret's coffee-coloured skin. Although their neighbour drew a pension, she conveyed an air of youth and glamour.

"So kind of you." Margaret beamed. "Well, I must take this troublemaker home."

"He's no trouble."

Sasha accepted the praise by licking Lucy's hand.

"Sasha is a she," Margaret explained. "Such a sweetheart, but a bit of a surprise. My son was offered a contract abroad at the last minute, so I agreed to look after her. I hope I won't regret it."

"I'm sure you won't. She's nice." Lucy suspected Sasha understood the compliments and enjoyed them.

"A Samoyed. They're a beautiful breed, and docile, but rather adventurous. She must have jumped over the wall to chase squirrels. Lucky she landed on your lawn. Well, I shall be rearranging my garden furniture so she can't do it again. See you at the carols."

Unexpectedly, Lucy felt a lump in her throat as she watched the dog trot cheerily away. The house seemed so quiet. She comforted herself by returning to her madrigals upstairs.

Wrapping didn't take long. While Lucy had saved money from her part-time job playing the piano for Margaret, most of it had been spent on charity. Goats for faraway strangers or a modest donation made a huge difference in Africa. Closer to home, a slice had gone to the local night shelter. If she'd had time, she would have volunteered there, but they were grateful for money too. She'd split the remaining cash between her mother, father and brother: one special thing each.

For Jennifer, Lucy had selected a silk scarf. Spotted in a charity shop, it boasted a designer label. Her mother would appreciate that. The marbled effect, shades of blue blurring together, would suit Jennifer's platinum hair. Best of all, the material would feel soft against Jennifer's skin.

There were malt whisky miniatures for Sebastian. Her father's first love was the books heaped on shelves throughout the house, but he was so particular about them that Lucy couldn't choose another with confidence. Sebastian read about metaphysics, moral dilemmas and the works of famous, infamous and obscure philosophers. These tomes were the tools of his trade as a professor of moral philosophy. He enjoyed sipping Scotch as he studied late into the evening.

Finally, she folded pretty paper around a Tupperware box. What do you give the man who has everything money can buy? She hoped she'd found the answer with the truffles she'd made from Fairtrade chocolate. Lucy had even limited her testing to one intense mouthful.

The doorbell rang as she snipped the last piece of ribbon. Lucy hurried to the front of the house, where Daniel's old room had been dusted and aired in readiness. She slid open a sash window to yell at the visitor. "I'm coming."

"And I'm waiting, Miss. I need your signature."

It wasn't the postman, but an old fellow from a private delivery company. He looked as exhausted as Lucy felt by the time she'd dashed down two flights of stairs. She was gripped by a rush of sympathy.

"Busy day?"

"Busy month. Sign here." He passed a handheld terminal to her, then gestured to the two large boxes at his feet. "Who's the lucky one? Flowers and booze, at a guess. Want me to bring them inside for you?"

"Yes, please. Can you leave them near the stairs?" The labels, addressed to 'The Freeman Family', gave no hint at the contents or their sender. This was an exciting surprise. She made a squiggle with the plastic stylus and handed the device back.

As soon as the delivery man had shuffled back to his van, Lucy attacked the boxes. The courier hadn't been wrong. She found a crate of champagne from Fortnum & Mason and a lavish arrangement of cream lilies tied with a gold ribbon. Drinking in the scent of the blooms, she noticed the gilt-edged envelope beside them.

Inside was a card, adorned with trumpet-wielding cherubs. 'To Mum, Dad and Lucy. With all my love, Daniel. Have a wonderful day. PS the flowers are your favourites, Mum – I remembered.'

Lucy clutched at the banister, giddiness enveloping her. The heady perfume must have overcome her, or perhaps it was despair. Once again, Daniel's absence would cast a cloud over Christmas. She would miss his witty anecdotes. Sebastian would be peeved. Jennifer, however, would be devastated.

Lucy acknowledged Jennifer would adore the flowers, though. Carrying them down to the kitchen, she arranged them in a crystal vase and brought them back to the ground floor. They would make a fine display on the marble console table in Jennifer's sitting room. Here, the décor was dramatic, bright colours evoking sea and sunshine. Sebastian had engaged local designers used by millionaires and several women with whom Jennifer had lunched in better days. Lucy recalled Sebastian complaining about the expense when Jennifer had hired them before. He had nevertheless sought out the firm when it became obvious that his wife must sleep downstairs. Maybe he felt sorry for her once her world shrank to a single floor of number 13. All she had was a bedroom at the quieter front of the building, her sitting room at the rear and a tiny wet room in between.

As Lucy thought, the blooms contrasted perfectly with the teal wallpaper. She positioned the vase next to solid gold statuettes of the three wise monkeys. Nicknamed Tom, Dick and Harry by Sebastian, they were another gift that had shown up one year instead of Daniel. He hadn't even bought them; in an unguarded moment, he'd admitted to Lucy that a rich superfan had given him the set.

A sudden feeling of outrage took her breath away. Why should she care so much? For most of her life, once fame had embraced Daniel and swept him away from Bristol, she'd hardly seen him. It wasn't as if he'd played a big part in her upbringing before then, either. Being ten years older, he'd mostly patronised her and enjoyed her hero worship. Once he'd set up the band, Lucy had been their greatest fan and gopher.

She'd idolised him. Her mother had too. Jennifer deserved more than trinkets, she needed to see her eldest child. On impulse, Lucy picked up the phone.

The call didn't go straight to voicemail as she'd expected.

"Hi, it's Dan."

"Daniel—"

"Oh, it's you, sis." His voice softened. "Thought it would be Dad, telling me I'm a naughty boy. What's up?"

23

"You're not coming."

"I just can't." There was a long pause. "You know how it is. When I see Mum, it's upsetting."

"No. I don't know. You haven't shown your face for over a year." Her words were bolder and sharper than she intended. She tried to sound placatory, to be the Lucy that both she and Daniel expected. "We all looked forward to your visit, and it would have been lovely for Mum. Flowers just aren't the same. Can't you see her for a couple of hours? Hop into one of your cars—"

He interrupted her again. "Sorry, no can do. I'm in Dubai. When you're offered megabucks to sing at a billionaire's party, you don't turn it down."

"Hire a private plane. I mean, if they're paying you so much, you can afford it."

"It won't work. I'll see you all another time." He sounded regretful and fatigued.

Annoyance fading, she said, "Soon, I hope."

"Me too. Are Mum and Dad around?"

"They're at Brian and Marilyn's." With luck, her parents would be tipsy when they returned. She would chill some of the champagne for them, too. A glass of fizz would soften the blow when they heard the news.

"Give them my love, won't you?"

24

"I will."

"Mwah, sis. Merry Christmas."

The phone clicked. Her brother's voice was replaced by a dialling tone. Lucy carried the champagne from the hall to the kitchen below. She placed two of the heavy bottles in the fridge and the rest in wine racks. It took several trips, meriting a treat afterwards.

She remembered the lovingly created truffles. Daniel wouldn't be eating them now. Lucy traipsed up to the top floor, her mood lifting as soon as she tore off the wrappings and sniffed the heavenly aroma of chocolate. Picking one up, she stared at it, then nibbled an edge. It was every bit as delicious as she expected. She crammed two into her mouth.

The sweetness and buttery texture set her pulse racing. Lucy took two more, relishing them as they melted. A sugar rush overwhelmed her, bringing a surge of confidence and pride. These were the best truffles in the world, and she had made them. She deserved to eat them all. Daniel most certainly didn't.

In minutes, the container was empty. Lucy ran the tip of her tongue over her lips to capture the last of the taste. Then she dashed to the hall, where the box of Milk Tray sat on the windowsill. How could it do any harm to take just one? Her heart thumped in her chest. She tore at the cellophane and cardboard until the top layer was gleaming before her, each chocolate like a brown jewel.

Which was best: strawberry, fudge, or orange? Maybe she should compare Cadbury's truffles with her own?

Her indecision lasted for a second. Lucy sampled all four flavours, then tried a praline. She giggled. Who needed champagne when lightness and brightness were only a chocolate away? She reached for one more, then another.

Half the layer was gone.

The buzz faded as quickly as it had engulfed her. With revulsion, she swallowed the last greasy, sugary remnants on her tongue. Her stomach churned at the thought of the calories.

Cooking would have to wait. She couldn't face the sight of food now. Lucy shivered. She threw the box in the bin and went back to her room, switching on her laptop for distraction. Maybe her friends could use help with 'Lord of the Rings Online'. She typed a message to Xander. "Cool Yule, X."

Within seconds, he replied. "MC."

"Short and sweet," she typed. "How's the raid?"

"Nearly over. I took a fireball. We're going to die." A moment passed before he added. "Without our favourite minstrel. Any chance you can get here?"

As she thought, they needed her. Xander's team missed her healing spells. Lucy's nausea eased. "Guess so," she typed. "Hang on one second."

The front door slammed. Sebastian called up the stairs, "Lucy, where are you? We have a crisis."

"Sorry. 600 seconds minimum," Lucy typed. She hated to let Xander down, but it seemed his group were as good as dead now. The sick feeling returned.

CHAPTER 3

NEIL

Bristol's Bridewell Police Station was not a cheerless place. Tinsel was draped around the incident room's whiteboard and Bing Crosby crooned through someone's laptop speakers. Nevertheless, the atmosphere remained tense. Neil Slater decided to compensate by reaching for the tin of Quality Street.

Sheridan Duffy turned the full force of her charm on him, a smile lighting up her pretty, heart-shaped face. "Pass them over here." She rolled the 'r'. Her accent, like those of most of his colleagues, was pure Bristolian.

"There aren't any green triangles left."

"I'll take my chances."

It was hard to say no to her. Since he met Gemma, Neil hadn't looked at another girl. Still, who could be blind to Sherry Duffy's golden hair and bubbly personality? More than that, she was his unofficial mentor. Although they were both detective constables, he'd only just joined the Major Crime Investigation Team, and she'd been there for a year.

He dropped a random handful of chocolates on the scratched white table that served as her desk. Glancing at the door, he said, "Well, Sherry, you've played this game before. Reckon we'll be home for Christmas?"

Sherry winced. "We can only keep Corbett for another two hours without charge. If he won't confess, who knows? I hope he does the decent thing. It's my turn to cook lunch this year. My mum and sisters won't take it kindly if I dump it on them at the eleventh hour."

"At least they'll have turkey. It's a nut roast for me at Gemma's."

She stared at him. "You wish. If our leave gets cancelled, you'll be lucky to get a Big Mac."

"A Maccy D's isn't so bad. I'd rather see Gems, though."

"Going to her parents for Christmas? You're behaving like a married couple."

Neil whispered, "Might be on the cards."

"No way! That's sudden." She added, "Hey, it can't be six months since you met her. And you're only twenty-three, right?"

Everyone stared at them. Neil immediately regretted saying a word. Sherry was like a megaphone in her excitement.

He was saved from having to explain. Detective Superintendent Ted Carter and Detective Chief Inspector Ab Ahmed burst through the door, faces beaming.

Sherry caught Neil's eye. He glanced around. The sense of relief in the room was palpable.

"Great news," Ted said. "Aaron Corbett has admitted killing the lad."

Neil found himself punching the air. "Yes!"

Ab's dark eyes glittered. "Won the sweep, have you?"

"Might have done." He was sure he'd been allocated 2 to 3pm on the twenty-fourth of December. He'd check Sherry's spreadsheet once the superior officers had left. Fate was on his side. Nobody would quiz him about Gemma when they'd just heard the news they'd hoped for.

A colleague looked up from his computer. "Guess we're all buying you drinks, Neil."

"Off to the pub later?" Ab asked.

"Sure. Want to come along, boss?"

"Sorry." Ab pulled a wry face. "I won't join you this time for my customary pint of lemonade. After all the hours we've been putting in, I owe it to my wife to relieve her of baby duty."

Ted chuckled. "Well done, Neil, and good work, everyone. It's as we thought. The youth was sent from London to sell Class A drugs. Aaron Corbett took exception to his presence. Fortunately, Corbett had the sense to confess in time for the holidays. I declare Christmas officially open." He held up a full carrier bag. It clanked as he flourished it. "There's a present for each of you."

"Not Chateau Counterfeit from Bedminster, surely, sir?" Ab teased.

"Very droll, Ab. Here's a clue, look." Ted pointed to the Tesco's logo on the bag. "The booze won't poison anyone and might even be drinkable. And before you say you don't indulge, there's a box of chocs in there for you."

"You spoil me, sir." Ab held up a hand. "Seriously, team, I'd echo what the Super says. It's been a hard case to work, and you all deserve your time off."

Ted doled out the bottles of wine. With a rugged face red from broken veins and a pot belly developing on his large frame, he'd clearly sampled more than the odd glass. "Prosecco for you, Sheridan. You like your fizz, I'm told?"

"Absolutely, sir."

"Have a Merry Christmas with your family, Sheridan."

"It'll be all the merrier now."

Ted's baggy eyes lit on Neil. "How about a nice bottle of red? Rioja."

"Perfect. Thanks, sir." He wasn't lying, but enthusiasm wouldn't hurt his career.

"Enjoy Christmas with your family, Neil."

"I'm spending the day with my girlfriend's folks."

Ted laughed. "Serious, is it?"

"Just the usual Christmas give and take," Neil said. "I'll go to my parents for the New Year. How about you, sir?"

"Off to my daughter's tomorrow," Ted said. "First, carols with my girlfriend in the Jackson Crescent gardens tonight. A Christmas Eve tradition, apparently."

"The most desirable post code in Bristol, isn't it?" Sherry said.

"How the other half live," Ab said.

"Jealous, are we?" Ted said, with good humour. "As it happens, I prefer the countryside myself."

A fragment of intuition teased at Neil's subconscious. He didn't know where Jackson Crescent was, couldn't recall visiting it or even hearing reports of a crime there. Yet he was suddenly gripped by a sense of menace.

He could hardly tell the Super. Ted would think he was mad.

"Are you okay, Neil?" Sherry's eyes were wide.

"I'm good." Neil realised he'd been frozen to the spot. He yawned and stretched his limbs. Why should he worry? Ted Carter was big and ugly enough to look after himself.

CHAPTER 4

LUCY

It had been a family custom for as long as Lucy could remember. From the beginning of December until Twelfth Night, the lantern stood on the windowsill in the hallway. As dusk fell, Sebastian would light it. The sole concession to the twenty-first century was the replacement of a wax candle by an LED lookalike.

Sebastian, his skinny figure enlarged by a padded jacket, hooked a finger through the ring at the top of the lantern. "Ready?"

Lucy nodded. Her father swung the lantern, sending swirls of red and green across the grey walls. He held the front door open.

She tilted Jennifer's wheelchair to push it over the threshold, then down the ramp onto the cobbled path. Her action was smooth; she had done this many times before. As far as she could tell, her mother was content. Lucy had done her best to ensure Jennifer was both well turned out and comfortable. Dark glasses with leopard spot frames added a touch of glamour and hid Jennifer's piercing stare. Lucy had also cleaned

34

her mother after the accident at Marilyn's and wrapped an incontinence pad in place, just in case.

"It's colder than I thought." Sebastian shivered. "Jen needs gloves."

"No, we won't be out that long. She had a manicure this morning and she'll want people to see, won't you, Mum?"

Jennifer whispered something unintelligible.

Sebastian seemed to understand her. "Very well, Jen. I'll get an extra blanket."

He returned to the hall, fetching a woolly throw from the whatnot. Shutting the door behind him, he tucked the covering protectively around his wife's legs. "There. I'll lead, shall I?"

Jackson Crescent's semi-circular garden had always reminded Lucy of a tangerine segment or a piece of Terry's Chocolate Orange. Number 13 was in a favoured position, its door opening onto the path that bounded the straight side of the mini-park. A roadway arced around the rest. Sleek, expensive cars were already parked there. The street itself was quiet. In contrast, a glow of light and babble of conversation rose from the central area.

Despite the excitement of the season, Lucy felt a sense of dread at meeting her neighbours. Jackson

Crescent was a place for high achievers. Even as a child, she hadn't been exempt from the pressure to succeed, and now she was merely tolerated as Jennifer's carer. Her playmates had moved on to fabulously successful jobs, and, as usual, she would have to listen to their parents boasting about them.

Sebastian would be modest. He still seemed surprised that his son was a rock star. Of course, where Lucy was concerned, he had no bragging rights.

He strode to the wrought iron gate that punctuated the hedge. "Make way for three more."

Following him, Lucy settled the wheelchair on flagstones near the gate. Although she'd worn wellington boots, venturing onto the lawn would be foolish. It was more mud than grass in the winter; Jennifer's weight would swiftly see the wheels get stuck.

"Mince pie?" Neighbourly Brian popped up like a grey-bearded jack-in-the-box. A baking tray appeared to float in front of him as he stepped out of the shadows. Lucy realised his hands were encased in black oven gloves.

"Yes, please." Lucy took one.

"I see Daniel isn't here yet," Brian observed.

"He can't make it after all," Sebastian said. "A diary clash."

Lucy was taken aback by the bitterness of his tone. He, too, must be upset on Jennifer's behalf. She comforted herself with the warm, sticky sweetmeat. "This is delicious, Brian."

"You don't want too many of those." The speaker was a man she didn't recognise. His broad, tall frame was bursting out of a dark wool overcoat. Having dropped his bombshell, he sipped from a chrome hip flask. Its contents lent his face a jovial, florid cast.

Hanging on his arm, another stranger giggled: a woman, thin, blonde and heavily made-up. She tottered on the edge of the flagstones, her stilettos unsuitable for the claggy ground.

Lucy felt heat rise to her cheeks. She was painfully aware they were already plump with pastry.

Brian rushed to the rescue. "It is Christmas, after all," he said, proffering his tray to the couple. "Incidentally, Lucy, Jennifer and Sebastian, have you met Zara yet? She's just moved in at number 7."

The red-faced man helped himself to a pie, while the woman waved dismissively at them.

"Pleased to meet you," she said, extending a gloved hand. Sebastian shook it.

After checking the chair's brakes had been applied, Lucy did likewise. Jennifer remained slack-jawed and immobile. It took a huge effort for her even to move a muscle; she must be conserving her strength.

"And this is?" Brian glanced in the direction of Zara's companion.

"Ted, my partner."

"Boyfriend." Ted clearly thought there was a difference.

"I'm Brian from the residents' committee." He shifted his grip on the tray and pumped Ted's hand enthusiastically. "Did Zara tell you? We organise Christmas carols in the garden every year. I did the lighting."

The trees, dotted around the edges of the lawn, were festooned with multi-coloured fairy lights.

"Well done, Brian. Your talents were wasted in IT." Zara's accent spoke of money, or elocution lessons, at least. "I bet that took you all day. Still, you've got plenty of time on your hands now you're retired, haven't you?"

"I wish someone would pay me to do nothing," Ted grumbled. "How on earth did you manage it? Those trees must be thirty feet high."

"It's simple. You tie a banana to a piece of string and throw that over first." Brian grinned.

Ted sneered. "The flying bananas of Jackson Crescent. So much for health and safety."

Sebastian sprang to his defence. "You can rely on Brian to be accurate. He was a fast bowler in his time."

"I might take it up again this summer. There's a veterans' cricket league." Brian brandished the tray in front of them again. "Do have more while they're hot. But watch out. I made these myself and used rather a lot of brandy. Don't drive afterwards." He winked at Ted.

Brian never took offence, did he? Still, Ted and Zara weren't trying to control his diet. Why was Lucy's weight any of their business? "Yes please, I'd love a second one," she told Brian.

"Good girl. Put a third in your pocket to have afterwards. There's a napkin." Brian nodded at the pile of serviettes on his tray. "Come on, Sebastian. Look, finish these off – Marilyn's just brought a heap out of the oven."

He pointed to his wife, easy to spot in a coat that matched her improbably red hair.

She beckoned to him.

"Must go."

Sebastian carefully wrapped the last pie, placing it in a pouch on the back of the chair. "I expect Jen would like that later. Darling, did you hear Brian? This is our new neighbour, Zara."

Jennifer's lips moved almost imperceptibly. No sound emerged.

Zara ignored her. "So how long have you lived here?" she asked Sebastian.

"Er, over thirty years. We moved in just before Lucy was born."

Lucy wished the carols would begin. She hated small talk as much as Sebastian. He, she knew, only suffered it so Jennifer would have an opportunity to socialise. That chance was rapidly receding. Zara clearly wasn't interested.

The slim blonde stared at Lucy for a brief, contemptuous moment, then flicked her eyes over the garden. Scores of Jackson Crescent residents were eating and chatting, but only the Freemans stood close by. Trapped on the flagstones by her shoes, Zara returned her focus to Sebastian. "And which house is yours?"

"Number 13."

"Oh, really? You're not superstitious, then." A glimmer of respect passed across her painted features.

"It's that large one at the end, isn't it?" Ted said. "I suppose they were more reasonable back in the day."

"Yes, well, I inherited it," Sebastian said. "Although I'd lived there before as a student, and then a junior lecturer. My uncle and aunt owned the property. They used to rent rooms out. I believe it was a wreck when they bought it, but they did it up."

"Could do with a lick of paint now, I see," Ted murmured. "I told you, Zara, these old properties are a money pit."

"I don't care. I like a place with character," Zara said.

Lucy almost warmed to her, until Zara spoiled it by adding, "I'd move if I were you, though, Sebastian. The three of you must be rattling around, and those stairs are tricky, surely?"

"We manage," Sebastian said.

"My brother used to live with us, too. He filled the space." It did feel empty without him, although Lucy should be used to it by now. He'd existed in a starrier universe for half her lifetime.

Zara opened her mouth to speak again and Lucy searched for a change of topic. Perhaps she could stop the interrogation and draw out a compliment for Jennifer. She stared pointedly at Zara's gels, gleaming under the lantern, and then at Jennifer's. "I love your nails," she said to Zara.

Zara simply replied, "Thanks," then began another question. "What—"

Marilyn came to the rescue. She bounded across the muddy lawn, flapping a sheaf of photocopied pages at them.

"There's a running order and lyrics," she said. "We'll begin with 'God Rest Ye Merry Gentlemen' once I've found Margaret Forsyth. Have you seen her?"

"No." Sebastian's eyes flicked around the throng before he waved a finger towards the gate. "There. Just coming in. With a dog."

Marilyn's smile slipped a fraction. "Dogs aren't allowed in the garden. She should know."

"Margaret probably doesn't." Lucy felt obliged to speak up. "She's just looking after Sasha for her son."

"Well —" Marilyn's words were drowned out by the cries of small children. They gathered around the fluffy white animal like bees to a honey pot.

Lucy was tempted to join them. In her opinion, Sasha was friendlier than most of the humans of Jackson Crescent.

"A Samoyed, isn't it?" Ted said. "What a handsome fellow."

"Sasha is a she," Lucy said.

Marilyn recovered her composure, her eyes twinkling as they settled on the youngsters. "I suppose we could make an exception for her today. Especially as Margaret is kindly leading the carols."

"Where's Margaret from?" Zara didn't sound thrilled. "She looks exotic."

Lucy couldn't avoid showing her disdain. "Bristol. Where else?"

"Her mother came from St Lucia," Sebastian said. "I suppose you might call it exotic. Jen was keen to go on holiday there at one time."

"Margaret has an incredible voice. You'll be impressed," Marilyn gushed. "She used to be a music teacher. Doesn't she give tuition now she's retired, Sebastian?"

Jennifer whimpered, distracting him. Zara and Ted diverted their attention to Sasha.

Lucy was silent. They wouldn't care about her part-time job helping Margaret with her lessons, so why should she tell them? She took the opportunity to examine the order of service. It was unchanged from the previous year, and probably the twenty before that.

Marilyn dashed off, distributing the few remaining sheets on her way to Margaret. There was a brief communication between them. Margaret, slim and elegant in her purple cape, nodded at Marilyn. Sasha caused a flurry of excitement at their feet. Finally, the infants were persuaded to stand still and stop stroking the animal.

Margaret began to sing, her honeyed soprano dominating the crowd as they joined in. Lucy held back from performing at full volume. This wasn't about her. Nevertheless, it was a magical experience to hear the melody rising into the air.

Jennifer made soft, incoherent sounds. Sebastian patted her hand. A toddler gawped at her, then tittered as the dog began to howl.

Lucy broke off from the carol. "Sasha is hopelessly out of tune. How will Margaret cope when her pupils return in the new year?" she said to her father, sotto voce.

Sebastian grinned. "Teaching the dog will be her ultimate challenge."

They sang 'Silent Night', 'Away in a Manger' and others so familiar that Lucy knew the words by heart. At last, Margaret announced the pièce de résistance, the 'Twelve Days of Christmas'.

"Let's practise the actions before we begin," she said. "What did my true love give to me on the first day of Christmas?"

There were whisperings between parents and children.

"A partridge in a pear tree," a small girl shouted.

"That's right, Evie. So when we sing about the partridge, I want you all to point to the old oak over there. Pretend it's a pear tree, okay? Now, who knows what happened on the second day?"

Finally, Margaret finished briefing the audience with appropriate words and actions. Dog, children and adults embarked on the song with gusto.

Lucy felt quite exhausted by the time they reached ten lords a-leaping. A token hop would have to suffice. She watched Sebastian and his fellow residents bounce up and down.

"That's worked off the mince pies," Sebastian panted. "Oh dear. What's going on?"

A hum needled its way into Lucy's consciousness, increasing in volume to a rumble. Margaret and the children around her wobbled as they mimed nine drummers drumming.

Margaret stopped singing. "Evie – move!" She shoved a child towards Sebastian.

Sasha barked, almost tripping Margaret as she grabbed the hands of two more infants and pulled them with her.

The flagstones trembled beneath Lucy's feet. A roar filled her ears, reaching its crescendo in a booming crash. She spluttered as a cloud of dust enveloped the garden. For a few seconds, it was all she could see.

When her vision cleared, the garden was perfectly still, apart from fairy lights flickering in four tall trees. She blinked. Shouldn't there be five? In the gloom, she made out a huge, dark shape lying on the ground. Lucy gasped. It was the sycamore which had stood in the corner near number 13. If the tree had toppled in the opposite direction, it would have smashed into her house.

Around her, Jennifer, Sebastian, and the rest of the throng were frozen like dun-coloured statues.

She sneezed, and the illusion shattered. Children began to sob and wail. The dog howled with them before deciding to whine at Margaret's feet instead.

Sebastian brushed the film of dust off his face. Tenderly, he did the same for his wife. "There's no need to worry, Jen. It's probably just a minor tremor. We'll go back inside and get you cleaned up."

He sounded confident, but Lucy supposed he was putting on a brave face. She shivered.

Margaret yelled above the din, "Keep away from that tree. The ground is unstable. Parents, count your children, please."

Ted raised an eyebrow. "Retired, is she? She's got you all under control." He added, "Thank goodness. We should still call the emergency services, though. Ah, Brian's on the case."

Brian, phone in hand, pointed its flashlight to the base of the fallen tree. A yawning black void occupied the corner of the garden, as if a giant had nibbled an edge of the tangerine segment.

"It's a sinkhole. Look," Brian said. "No wonder the tree came down."

The small girl, Evie, shrieked. "There's a skeleton."

The other children began to scream.

"Don't be silly, Evie," Lucy said. "Of course there isn't—" Then her gaze flicked from Sebastian's horrified face to the deep hole and the skull whose sightless eyes stared back at her.

She realised she was screaming too.

CHAPTER 5

LUCY

Sebastian shook Lucy's shoulders. "Don't scream," he said. "Please. It will upset Jen."

Lucy took a deep breath, grateful for the chilliness of the air as she gulped it down. "S-sorry."

"It's a shock, I know," Sebastian said. "Let's take your mum home."

"Wait." Ted, the policeman, pointed a finger at him. "You've lived here for years, haven't you? Would you be able to take a roll call, just to check no-one has fallen in that crater? I assume you know everybody."

"Margaret would be better placed for that." Sebastian gestured towards the retired teacher. "She appears to be doing an excellent job already. I really must see to my wife."

Zara, clinging to Ted's arm, sobbed through a mouthful of dust. "I can't believe there's a dead body yards from my flat. The estate agent said Bristol was safer than London."

Ted placed his other arm around her. "Don't worry," he said, with more warmth than Lucy would have expected of him. "You're okay. That's all that matters."

"What about him?" Zara pointed to the skeleton clearly visible in Brian's flashlight.

"Love, don't upset yourself. It may not be a man at all. Animal bones can look surprisingly human."

Zara didn't seem reassured. She coughed violently. Tears sent dirty streaks down her face.

Ted gave her a squeeze. "Get back inside and pour yourself a large glass of wine. Christmas or no, I'll call in favours and get an opinion from a forensic specialist. And you can absolutely believe your estate agent. Our homicide rate is only one-third of London's. All right?"

She nodded.

"Off you go, then. I'll see you later." He slapped her skinny rump.

Margaret was shepherding the crowd towards the gate. The jolliness of carols and mince pies had been forgotten. A sea of subdued faces eddied and swirled around Lucy as she clutched the wheelchair. Even the dog was silent.

Ted caught Margaret's eye. "Is everyone present and correct?"

"Yes, I think so. Luckily, I stood in the centre of the garden to lead the singing, and the others gathered around me. All the parents have located their children and there are no stray adults except Brian." She gestured to the grey-bearded man standing by the edge of the sinkhole. His phone was now clamped to his ear.

"I hope he's calling the emergency services," Ted said.

"I believe he is." Margaret turned away to marshal the Jackson Crescent residents.

"I'll have a word with him."

Lucy watched Ted stride across the muddy lawn. She, Sebastian, and Jennifer weren't going anywhere fast. They could only push the wheelchair home once the queue through the gate had subsided.

Brian looked up at Ted's approach. "Can you tell them, please?" He spoke into his phone again. "As I was saying, a huge crater has appeared in the gardens of Jackson Crescent. I am not drunk, I'm afraid."

"No problem. Give it to me." Ted held his hand out.

"You can talk to one of your colleagues," Brian said, before passing him the mobile.

Ted smiled broadly into the phone. "It's Detective Superintendent Ted Carter," he said. "Who do I have the pleasure of speaking to?"

Lucy heard him say there was a sinkhole, and he was helping to clear the scene. He would take a few photographs for forensics. The flashlight, still switched on, illuminated the fallen tree as he gave his report.

Sebastian picked up his lantern and eased past the stragglers. "I'm going to take a closer look."

"Not too close," Brian waved him away. "I'm sure I saw bricks. That's definitely a collapsed cellar, and we don't know how far it extends."

Lucy shivered. "More of it could cave in."

"Exactly," Brian agreed. "We can expect a wrangle with the council over liability. I wonder if it's attached to one of the houses? It's right outside yours."

"I don't know anything about it," Sebastian said.

Lucy gaped at her father, then quickly closed her mouth, hoping Brian hadn't noticed. While she wanted to forget everything that had ever happened in the cellar, she hadn't expected Sebastian to lie.

Dissembling was, however, an art in which Sebastian excelled. Lucy believed this was because he so rarely did it. Her father only stretched the truth when it was fundamentally important to him, somehow keeping his body language as transparent and honest as ever. All who knew him commended him on his frankness. They treated him like an open book, although not necessarily one they understood.

Jennifer muttered a few garbled syllables.

"What's Jen trying to tell us?" Brian asked.

"She's worried about our home," Sebastian replied. He patted his wife's shoulder. "Don't fret, darling. I'll go back and check it over."

"Be careful," Brian urged his retreating figure, adding to Lucy, "I'm sure your house will be fine. The hole doesn't seem to stretch under the path towards it."

Jennifer continued to mumble. Lucy held her hand. It was the only comfort she could offer as she watched Ted barking orders and a stream of carollers leaving the garden. Eventually, the dog settled at Jennifer's feet, quietening her. The flow of babble stopped.

"Margaret?" Lucy realised her neighbour was no longer in view. Only Brian and Ted remained in the garden.

"I expect she's forgotten." Brian petted the animal. "I'll take Sasha round to Margaret's, Lucy. You've got your hands full."

"We'll do it. You want to make sure that policeman doesn't walk off with your phone." Sebastian had returned. "The house is perfectly sound, I'm pleased to say. As I pointed out earlier, that cellar isn't ours."

The dog looked up at Lucy.

"What a relief," Lucy murmured, dropping to her knees to cuddle Sasha. She exhaled, suddenly aware of the tension leaving her body. "I wish we had a dog. Could we, Dad? It would be more company for Mum."

"Lucy, not now." Sebastian's tone was sharp. "We've got too much to deal with. The last thing we need is you acting like a silly child. You know you've never kept a pet alive for more than a fortnight." His gaze rested on Jennifer, as if surprised that his wife had survived for so long in Lucy's care.

He must have noticed Lucy's lips tighten, for he said, "I'm sorry. I didn't mean to sound harsh, but you remember what happened to your guinea pig, don't you? And even the goldfish only lasted a week."

Lucy's eyes grew hot. She knelt down, burying her face in the soft, fluffy fur on Sasha's back until the animal pulled away.

CHAPTER 6

NEIL

Neil's stomach was pleasantly full as he drove away from Glastonbury. Gemma's family ran a vegan bed and breakfast in an old coaching inn just outside the town. While they were closed for Christmas, her mother was used to cooking substantial breakfasts. The Quorn sausage, mushrooms and beans were nearly as good as the real thing.

Somerset roads were quiet on this Boxing Day morning. He had the pleasure of overtaking a tractor on a straight stretch, enjoying the acceleration from his nippy Peugeot RCZ. The insurance was crippling, but he loved the car's sporty looks and power. It didn't take long to hit the M5 motorway and let the engine purr.

His feelings were bittersweet. Christmas with Gemma had been idyllic until the moment she'd turned him down. He hadn't even intended to pop the question so soon. There had been a cheap costume ring in his Christmas cracker, and he'd suspected a hint; the crackers appeared home-made. The opportunity was too good to miss. As it happened, the ring couldn't have been Gemma's idea at all. She treated it as a big joke. Luckily, he had proposed in private, not in front of the whole clan.

Later, she'd apologised. They'd talked for hours in her room, a cheese plant throwing huge shadows on the candlelit walls. Like the rest of the house, her space drew him in. Gemma said the place was comfortable because it was built on ley lines. They'd sat on her pine bed, holding hands, while she told him to live for the moment rather than plan the future. Neil had a high-flying career in Bristol ahead of him, she explained, while she was a country girl at heart. Then she'd kissed him and they'd made love.

Being with her seemed natural, as if it was always meant to be. He just needed to persuade her. Already, Neil missed the scent of lavender, the softness of Gemma's black hair and the feeling of drowning in her sea-green eyes.

Leaving the M5, he shook away the memory of rejection, suddenly relieved that he'd been given a Boxing Day shift. He zipped along roads that normally showed red on Google Maps, arriving in Bristol city centre in a matter of minutes. The concrete multistorey carpark was seldom so empty. He'd brought his gym kit, hoping to work out with Ab as usual, but the building was closed. However, Ab was waiting when he walked into the CID office at Bridewell.

"How's things, boss?"

Ab laughed, his perfect teeth white against his brown skin. "I've come in for a rest. The baby's teething. Listen, an interesting job has come up. Probably nothing to it, though. A dead body in Clifton."

"That's big news, surely? In a posh area like that, the murder rate isn't exactly high."

"Correct. But I'm guessing this corpse has been there a hundred years. It turned up in one of those old Georgian streets and there's not much left of it. A sinkhole opened in a garden, and they found a skeleton." Ab sipped a Starbucks coffee. "The CSIs are there and they've just sent footage across. Want to look?"

Neil watched the short video on the DI's monitor. First, the camera panned out to show a fallen tree and the adjacent sinkhole. This was an enormous crater, roughly circular. Zooming closer, roots could be seen poking out at a crazy angle. Finally, the photographer focussed on the void. Here, far below ground level, the skeleton sat beneath a crumbling brick archway. The crime scene investigators had used floodlights. Under their powerful illumination, the bones were bleached white, recognisable despite the soil strewn over them.

"What is this place? It's like something out of a horror movie." The video did have a filmic quality, giving Neil a sense of detachment. On the rare occasions he'd seen corpses before, they'd been flesh and blood, their deaths horribly real.

"It's a collapsed cellar in Jackson Crescent. Where SuperTed's girlfriend lives. He was with her when it happened. It may have been Christmas Eve and he might even have been drinking, but he had everyone away from the scene in minutes. He personally took photos to get confirmation the remains were human. Which, unfortunately, they are."

"No doubt about that, surely?" Neil stared at the pale bones. "Maybe SuperTed sang carols with a murderer."

"That's not funny." Despite his words, Ab grinned. "Don't jump the gun. It may not be a murder."

"If it wasn't, wouldn't someone report a dead body in their cellar?"

"You'd think so. But here's the thing. Like all the best addresses in Clifton, Jackson Crescent has a garden in the centre. It's owned by the council and the cellar sits under there. When you make enquiries, ask where the access is. The CSIs may find the way in, of course, but it's likely to take them a while. There are health and safety issues. Although we've secured the site, we're still working with the council to make it free from danger."

"What do we know about the deceased, Ab?"

Ab frowned. "Only that they're dead. That's it. Initial indications say the remains are a young adult, but that's being confirmed. Gender is probably male, but again, we need forensics to confirm that. They can also tell us how long the bones were underground. If it's more than seventy years, we'll be handing them over to the archaeologists. For now, we're treating it as a potential crime scene. Ted wants someone to go to Jackson Crescent ASAP to reassure his girlfriend that we're on the case. So I need you and Sherry to see her. She's Zara Greely at number 7. While you're there, you can visit a couple of other concerned members of the public."

"And they are?"

"Brian Parton. Number 14. He's the guy who dialled 999. According to Ted, he knows everything going on in Jackson Crescent. He'll be expecting you. And Sebastian Freeman, opposite the sinkhole, who won't be."

Neil found Sherry by the coffee machine.

"Third cup of the day," she explained. "Have you seen Ab?"

"Yes. We're off to Jackson Crescent. You're not hung over, are you?"

There was no hint of it in Sherry's peachy complexion, but make-up hid a lot of sins. Besides, she didn't normally drink so much coffee.

Sherry shook her head. "I'm good. Did she say yes?"

"Not exactly."

Sherry winced supportively. "Maybe you need to be patient. You're still friends?"

"Yes."

"Don't give up, then. Whose car are we taking today? Dear me, I left my Porsche at home. Guess it's your boy racer."

She was unusually quiet as Neil drove to Clifton, a state of affairs which suited him. He'd been dreading more questions about his proposal. Instead, he mused about the Super's girlfriend and her Christmas surprise. Small wonder Ted Carter was throwing resources at Jackson Crescent.

A fine drizzle of rain was falling, just between two stops on his windscreen wipers. Neil erred on the side of caution, suffering a scraping sound across his screen in the interests of visibility. The paintwork of Clifton's pricy houses, better maintained than inner city Bedminster where he lived, gleamed beneath a slick of moisture.

The journey was short. Their destination lay not far from the centre of Bristol, having been built for wealthy citizens many years before the twentieth century's urban sprawl. Bedminster's boxy cottages were dwarfed by these substantial stone villas. Neil passed a row of shuttered boutiques and bars in the area called The Village, then drove down long, straight Jackson Road. Just before the first turning into Jackson Crescent, he parked behind an Aston Martin DBS.

It was a beautiful car, absolutely spotless. Neil risked a covetous glance, but Sherry paid no attention to it. Instead, she pointed across the way to a large van with a prominent logo. "Uh oh, the BBC are here."

"And Sky," Neil said, as they rounded the corner. The commercial station's vehicle was just inside the crescent itself.

This was an upmarket street. Although terraced, the whitewashed houses were four storeys high. This was easier to see at the back, in Jackson Road. Only three floors were visible at the front until you realised that each had a set of steps down to a basement level, and presumably a second front door.

"I'd love a flat here," Sherry said. "Imagine the rent, though."

"You don't pay any to your mum and dad, do you? A touch more affordable."

She laughed. "Much."

While their individual footprints were modest, the properties were grouped around a central garden, a semi-circle enclosed by a hedge. Neil noticed this was surrounded by sections of steel mesh beribboned with crime tape. By the furthest corner, a cluster of reporters were interviewing a blonde woman in leather trousers.

"A celeb?" he asked Sherry.

She laughed. The icy rain seemed to be waking her up. "Don't think so. Z-list at best," she said, peering at the gathering.

"Ab didn't mention a media strategy."

"It's no comment from us. Anyhow, they don't know who we are. Let's take a look around; see the lie of the land before we meet Ms Greely."

Despite the weather, a crowd of onlookers had gathered. Most were watching the reporters. Others stood around the perimeter of the garden in ones and twos, squinting through gaps in the metal barriers and hedge. The DCs followed suit.

A large white tent covered almost half of the garden. The uprooted tree lay next to it. Nearby, a young man in a hi-vis jacket was arguing with a CSI in protective clothing. Their body language suggested the CSI was winning.

"Should we help our lad?" Neil asked.

"The site's under control. Leave them to it. Let's find number 7." Sherry glanced at the nearest house. "It'll be on this row."

Neil followed her, passing number 1, and then 2 next door. The odd and even numbers weren't separated. At their destination, he picked his way past stone urns, carved angels, and pots of herbs in a flagged front yard. Several steps led up to a solid wooden door, panelled and painted a glossy navy blue. An array of buttons suggested there were three flats. Zara's name wasn't listed against any of them.

"Sure this is the right place?" he asked.

"Definitely. Ab wouldn't get it wrong. Look, there's a basement. We'll try that."

A wooden plaque, shaped like a hand with a pointing finger, announced that a garden apartment was located down a flight of stairs. Neil's smart shoes slipped on the wet stone steps. He clung to a handrail as Sherry descended briskly in front of him. They found a less grand door with a lattice of windowpanes, each sprayed with artificial snow. There was no slot for letters. Instead, a grey tin mailbox protruded from the wall, a neat sign stating it belonged to Z Greely.

Sherry rang the bell, waiting thirty seconds and then knocking on the door as well for good measure. Neil tapped on a sash window to the side. Nothing happened.

"She must be out," Sherry said. "Brian Parton next. Fancy squeezing past the reporters at the end of the path?"

"No," Neil admitted.

"Me neither. We'll go the long way round."

Walking the length of the crescent gave Neil the opportunity to peek at the residents' cars. Among the Mercedes estates and Range Rovers, he spotted a silver Lotus Elise with a personalised plate: ZG7. Zara couldn't be far.

"I wonder what's happening at number 14." Sherry nodded towards a corner house on the other side of the road from the straight row. It was set apart from the others in a neatly clipped shrubbery behind wrought iron railings. A grey-bearded man, his parka keeping the rain at bay, lounged outside its black metal gate. He was in rapt conversation with two elderly women, umbrellas clashing.

"So it could be a Frenchman?" one of them said.

"Definitely. We took hundreds of PoWs in the Napoleonic Wars." The man's voice reminded Neil of a school teacher. He didn't sound local.

"Excuse me." Neil marched around the trio and signalled to the gate. The umbrellas swivelled and quivered. A thick droplet splashed in Neil's eye.

The bearded fellow stepped to one side. "This is my house. Can I help?"

"You're Brian Parton?"

"The very same. And you would be…?"

"DC Neil Slater." Neil showed Brian his warrant card. "And this is my colleague, DC Sheridan Duffy. I understand you reported an incident on Christmas Eve. Can we go inside to discuss it, please?"

"Of course. I've been waiting for you. Nice talking to you, ladies."

As Brian unlocked his front door, Sherry complimented him on the wreath that adorned it. It was a circle of holly, ivy and pine cones tied with tartan ribbons.

"Thank you," Brian said. "I fear we are quite competitive about Christmas in Jackson Crescent."

Neil's attention was distracted by the umbrella-wielding bystanders. He heard one sightseer say to the other, "This is my first sinkhole."

"Mine too. What a lovely man."

"I wonder why the police want him."

"Do you think—"

The words were cut off when the detectives stepped inside Brian's Minton-tiled hallway, closing the heavy door.

"Had Jackson Crescent been built by the Napoleonic Wars?" Sherry asked.

"I shouldn't think so," Brian said. "This would have been fields in the early nineteenth century. It's fun winding up the grockles, though. Anyway, the Empress Eugenie used to live round the corner."

"Really?" Sherry asked.

Neil looked sharply at both of his companions. "You don't need to keep up the story. I'm not a tourist."

"And I'm not lying to you. Check Wikipedia later. Meanwhile, I'm guessing you could use some coffee. I have a rather good espresso machine. Do you take milk?"

"Neil does. I'd love mine black." Sherry flashed her brightest smile.

Divested of his parka, Brian was revealed as having an athletic build. He was wearing cargo pants and a blue T-shirt bearing the legend 'Nil illegitimi carborundum'. "You understand Latin?" he asked.

Sherry giggled. "Don't let the whatsits grind you down."

"Indeed. It's a mantra that has served me well. I spent forty years in IT. I've even done some work on the police national computer, but I can't say what. They made me sign the Official Secrets Act." Brian tapped his nose.

The kitchen, gleaming with chrome and white marble, was off the hallway. A shelf festooned with pots of living herbs added a homespun touch reminiscent of Gemma's place, but that was the only similarity. Whereas Gemma had made a career of upcycling old furniture, here everything was new and highly engineered. It was clean, too, unlike the cottage Neil shared with two of his university friends.

Four tall stools were arranged in a precise row below a marble breakfast bar. Brian pulled three out, setting them in another neat line. "Sit down."

Neil watched with interest as Brian pressed a silvery machine's buttons and levers. Beans disappeared from a hopper at the top, resurfacing as hot coffee in china cups. Brian hissed steam through a milk jug, adding the result to two of the drinks with a flourish. "Enjoy." He pulled up a seat next to Sherry. "Now, you had some questions."

"I'll take notes if I may, and email a statement to you afterwards," Sherry said. "Is that all right?"

"Of course. I'm more than happy to help." Brian steepled his hands under his chin.

Sherry removed her laptop from its bag. "Just booting up."

"If it's slow, let me know. I might be able to suggest something," Brian said.

"Thanks, but there's no need. Ready now."

"I'll start then. Tell me about this sinkhole." Pleasantries over, Neil took the lead. They had an informal arrangement: Sherry quizzed the women, and Neil, the men. Sherry wasn't averse to chipping in with a comment, though, even playing the dumb blonde if she thought it would get quicker answers.

That wasn't necessary here. Brian was keen to talk. "It's technically a collapsed cellar. Despite the yarns I spin for the day-trippers, I didn't know it was there until Christmas Eve."

"What happened?"

"There was a group of us singing carols in the garden. Including a very senior policeman, I should add. Suddenly, we heard a thunderous crash. The ground shook, and we found ourselves staring into the abyss. I'm afraid to say that a dead man stared right back."

Sherry looked up from her laptop. "That must have been a terrible shock for you. Was anyone hurt?"

"Luckily not. Nobody was standing in that spot, or under the tree that fell. Your colleague did a splendid job of clearing the garden. Safety is still a concern, naturally." Brian winced. "The council's emergency response team sent someone to inspect the other trees. They don't think there's an immediate threat. I hope they do a proper investigation soon."

"How many people were present for the carols?" Neil asked.

"A few dozen. It could have been a bloodbath, couldn't it? Sorry, that was in poor taste, given the fate of that hapless fellow in the cellar. It is a chap, I assume?"

"I can't say." Sensing a twinge of disappointment from Brian, Neil added, "I'm not being evasive. Tests are necessary to determine gender. They're in progress."

"Yes, I've seen your CSIs. They should be on danger money. Suppose the earth moves again?"

"It might help if we could gain access to the site from another direction. Do you know of a way into the cellar?"

"No, I don't." Brian was emphatic. "Nor do Sebastian and Lucy Freeman, who live across the path from it, at number 13. They've been there forever, but they weren't even aware a cellar existed under the garden. Sebastian won't be keen to lay claim to it, either. We all want the council to pay for repairs."

CHAPTER 7

NEIL

The Z-list celebrity was no longer in sight, but a cameraman and several reporters stood outside number 13. They swooped on Neil and Sherry like vultures. A microphone was thrust in Sherry's face, no doubt because she was the more photogenic.

"Do you live here?"

Sherry cast her eyes down.

"No." Neil answered for her.

"How do you feel about a murder in Clifton?"

"Sorry, we need to get out of the rain. We can't talk." Deciding he was justified in taking liberties, Neil grabbed Sherry's hand, pulling her into the front yard of number 13. They were close to the CSIs here, separated only by a strip of cobbled path and the hedge. Neil reminded himself to ask the Freemans about access to the collapsed cellar.

Dragging Sherry with him, Neil cleared the flagged yard in two strides, passing stone steps down to the basement. He noted metal furniture and pots of shrubs. They were eerily familiar, and he struggled to understand why. Nothing else about the house was exceptional. It was typical of the area: tall, white, and screaming of money. The red door sported a festive wreath even showier than Brian's, in this case, a hoop of gold tinsel entwined with winking LEDs.

Sherry pulled her hand away.

"No offence meant," Neil said hastily.

"None taken."

The bell was answered by a woman with wavy fair hair in a messy bun. It was impossible to guess either her age or dress size. She wore a food-stained black smock and no make-up. Her sky-blue eyes were dull with resignation.

"I've already said I don't know anything." Her voice, pleasant and melodious, was free of rancour. While she looked like a cleaner or childminder, she was also what Neil's mother would describe as well spoken.

Sherry discreetly flashed her warrant card. "We're not reporters."

Neil copied her. "We'd like to see Sebastian and Lucy Freeman about the sinkhole."

"I'm Lucy. Come on in. My mother also lives here. Jennifer Freeman. I expect she'll want to see you, too."

Neil caught Sherry's eye. She nodded.

73

Lucy ushered them through the hall to a sitting room furnished in tones of teal and mustard. There were matching ornaments on a deep green fir tree standing proud by the window. It reached almost to the ceiling. A pleasant pine scent permeated the air.

Neil clocked Sherry marvelling at it, no doubt wondering how Brian could beat that. They hadn't seen his Christmas tree, but it was bound to be spectacular.

Lucy noticed their attention. "Dad always chooses a real tree for my mother."

A woman sat with her back to them in a tan leather wing chair, apparently staring out of the window. Lucy darted around to face her.

"Mum? These are two police detectives. Neil and Sheridan." Lucy sounded breathless, as though their visit was an exciting treat she wanted to share. She beckoned to the DCs to join her.

Sherry smiled. "Good to meet you, Jennifer. Please call me Sherry."

In contrast to Lucy's volubility, Jennifer simply grunted. Unnervingly, she continued to gaze outside.

Under the window, a console table held statues of three wise monkeys, their golden finish gleaming in the sun's rays. A trick of the light gave two the appearance of staring back at the older woman. The third figurine, hands over eyes, merely listened.

"You've spotted Tom, Dick and Harry," Lucy said. "They were a present from my brother."

"How thoughtful. They suit your colour scheme," Sherry said.

Jennifer croaked out a syllable which might have been 'yes'. Despite her strange behaviour, she cut a dash, as smart as her daughter was unkempt. There was no dirt on the green velvet lounging pyjamas, which fitted Jennifer's figure well. Her neat platinum hair showed a mere hint of grey at the roots, her fingernails manicured, her lips glossed. Close up, it was possible to catch a whiff of perfume.

Sherry noticed. "What a lovely fragrance. Is it Issey Miyake, Jennifer?"

Lucy nodded.

"My mum adores it too." Sherry fixed her eyes on Jennifer's stare. "We'd like to ask a few questions, Jennifer. Neil will take notes on his computer."

"All right if we sit here?" Neil gestured to a sofa beside the table.

"Yes," Lucy said, "but Mum can't tell you much."

"Every little helps," Sherry said.

Neil switched on his laptop. It didn't boot up as swiftly as Sherry's. He suspected the IT helpdesk had been charmed into giving her a better machine.

"I'm afraid we need to speak to your mother privately," Sherry told Lucy. "Would you mind leaving the room for a few minutes, please? Perhaps we can have a chat with you afterwards."

"Actually, she can't speak." Lucy's voice was gentle. "Mum has Parkinson's. Quite badly, as a matter of fact. It's a version called PSP, or progressive supranuclear palsy."

"Is that right?" Sherry asked Jennifer.

The older woman's chin wobbled. She wheezed out a groan.

"I think we could talk to Lucy first, couldn't we, Neil? Can we have a word with you alone, please, Lucy?"

"Maybe in the kitchen?" Lucy said.

Unlike Brian's house, the kitchen at number 13 was on the floor below. Neil had more of an opportunity to appraise the décor in the hallway. It was stuffy and formal, enlivened only by swags of festive tinsel. The walls were grey, a shade picked out in fleur-de-lys shapes on the mustard-hued carpet. Gold-framed oil paintings portrayed men, women and children in the clothes and hairstyles of bygone centuries.

"Ancestors?" he asked.

Lucy tittered nervously. "Mum bought them at auction, or her interior designer did. She likes strong colours, though. She says they're what the Georgians used when the houses were built."

"I thought she couldn't speak?"

"She hasn't always been like this," Lucy said in a low voice. "Ten years ago, her balance started to go. Now, she can't talk, or move her eyes, or – never mind."

"It must be difficult for you," Sherry said sympathetically.

"It's worse for her." Lucy flushed.

They descended the stairs to another lobby. With a jolt, Neil realised a man was waiting for them.

Lucy seemed surprised too. She almost stumbled on the last step. "Er, Neil and Sherry – this is my dad, Sebastian. Dad – DC Neil Duffy and Sheridan Slater, from Avon and Somerset Police."

"It's Sherry Duffy and Neil Slater," Sherry corrected her. "Don't worry, Lucy. We get confused ourselves."

Neil had assumed from Brian's comment that Sebastian and Lucy were a couple. Now he saw them together, it was obvious they were father and daughter. The resemblance was striking despite Lucy's chunkiness. Sebastian was skinny and stooped. He wore expensive versions of the smart casual clothes Neil favoured for work: a charcoal jacket, blue shirt, and cream chinos.

"How can I assist you, officers?" Sebastian's eyes, spookily identical to Lucy's, swept over the visitors.

"It's about the sinkhole," Neil said.

"I may not be much help, I'm afraid. I heard, felt, and saw the collapse in that order. Come into my study and we'll have a word. Lucy, can you get us all coffee, please?"

Sebastian's thinning grey hair echoed his wife's roots, leading Neil to suspect that Lucy was around thirty or forty, and old enough not to take orders from her father. Lucy nevertheless nodded meekly and asked who would like milk and sugar.

"Thank you, I'll take it black." Sherry was quick to accept her fifth caffeine shot of the day.

"No coffee, thanks, Lucy. Sorry, I'll see you later." Neil followed Sebastian and Sherry through the lobby to the front of the house. He noticed that the door to the outside world was completely blocked by a tall bookcase.

More books filled Sebastian's study. It resembled a library, shelves reaching to the ceiling. They were full to bursting. Other tomes sat in piles on the parquet floor and the leather-topped desk.

"Have you got enough to read?" Neil asked, tongue firmly in cheek.

"Probably not." Sebastian seemed perfectly serious. "In my view, you can never read enough."

Neil glanced at the titles. "Philosophy?" he hazarded.

"Yes," Sebastian admitted. "I'm a professor of moral and political philosophy at the university." He sat behind the desk, stretched his legs, then pointed to a pair of chairs. They were upholstered in a dark blue print to match what little could be glimpsed of the wall. "Take a seat."

Neil pulled his closer to the desk, disturbing a wedding photograph perched on a corner. He put out a hand to catch it.

The couple smiled out of the ornate gold frame, sunlight haloing their fair heads. Smart in a suit and tie, the groom was recognisable as Sebastian, despite his droopy moustache. Jennifer wore her hair short and her meringue dress long. She was visibly pregnant and very young.

Sherry glanced at it. "I'm a sucker for a wedding picture. That was taken at Christ Church in Clifton, wasn't it?"

"Yes," Sebastian said. "The happiest day of my life. Call me sentimental if you wish."

"How old were you?" Sherry asked.

"Twenty-eight. Jen was twenty." Sebastian gazed tenderly at the photo. "I was a junior lecturer then. She was one of my students."

Sherry retained an expression of polite interest. Neil thought he had managed to do the same, but Sebastian coughed awkwardly.

"I know that sort of relationship would be forbidden now. Thank goodness we got together in different times. I've never met anyone like her. Such beauty and energy. Did you notice her sales awards?"

"Yes," Sherry said. "On the wall in the lounge upstairs."

They had only been there two minutes ago, yet Neil still found it hard to recollect anything but paintings on display. Finally, he dredged up a memory of framed certificates and a tall, slim woman shaking hands with a man in a suit.

"Jen worked in publishing, on the academic side. She loved it. It's a shame she had to retire early."

"I gather she's unwell," Neil said.

"Sadly. I'm lucky Jen's still around. Did Lucy explain about PSP? Most sufferers would have died years ago. It's only Jen's drive that keeps her going." A shadow flitted across Sebastian's face.

Sherry showed him her laptop. "I'll be taking notes and will make sure you get a copy to review."

"Sounds good. You can email me at the university." Sebastian handed her a business card.

"I take it this is your cellar?" Neil asked, trying to figure out if the hole in the garden was on the same level.

Sebastian shook his head. "No. This is the basement. We do have a cellar underneath, but we don't use it."

"So, there's another floor below this one? Might we have a look, please?"

"I'm sorry. As I said, we never use it. The door's locked and I can't even remember where the key's gone." Sebastian's wide-eyed, open body language suggested he was telling the truth.

"Can you get through from it to the cellar that collapsed?"

"Definitely not. You may be able to crawl in via the sewers or something. I've never tried to go near it and I told Jen, Daniel, and Lucy not to do so either."

This raised two avenues of discussion. Neil began to explore the first. "Who is Daniel?"

"My son. Our eldest child. He used to live with us, but he flew the nest when his band took off. You may have heard of Dr Sweet?"

Before Neil could admit he hadn't, Sherry interrupted. "Have I ever? My mum's mad about them. The best Britpop band of all time, according to her. She's even got a photo signed by Daniel and Jason."

Sebastian looked impressed. "That could be valuable. I imagine it's quite rare. Jason Jardine left Dr Sweet just before they made the charts."

"With 'Getting High'. I sang that tune non-stop as a kid. So catchy." Sherry hummed it. "See, I'm a fangirl too. Of course, I didn't know what the lyrics meant."

"Unfortunately, drugs got the better of at least one member of the group. It's a terrible shame. Such nice lads." Sebastian's eyes flicked to his left, evidently recalling them. "Not everyone can cope with fame."

"They split up when Gaz died, didn't they?"

Sebastian nodded. "Yes. After Gareth Fields' heroin overdose, Daniel decided to do his own thing. He always hated drugs." There was a slight tremor in his voice. Perhaps he was trying to convince himself, or simply felt sorry for the dead bandmate.

It was understandable that Daniel would avoid drugs after his friend's overdose. Neil recalled his second year at university, when he'd shared a party lifestyle with three flatmates. He still lived with two of them. The third hadn't survived the year, victim of a batch of bad pills at a rave. You didn't need to be a stressed superstar to make a fatal decision.

Sherry was staring at him. She knew the story and had probably guessed his thoughts.

"Daniel has made a success of his solo career since, I'm pleased to say," Sebastian continued.

Forcing himself to focus, Neil made a mental note to ask for Daniel's contact details later. He returned to the other point that had grabbed his attention. "Your neighbour mentioned you'd lived in Jackson Crescent for a long time."

"That's right. I lodged here as a young man, then we all moved into the house when Jen was pregnant with Lucy, over thirty-two years ago. In between, when Daniel was small, we lived in Singapore."

"How did you find out about the cellar under the garden?"

Sebastian answered coolly. "My uncle mentioned rumours. He used to own this house, by the way. He had no idea why a cellar was built there, and neither have I."

"Who might be able to help with that?"

"You'd have to ask the council."

"I believe you saw the body in there. Do you know the identity of the deceased?"

"Again, I have absolutely no idea. It goes without saying I had no knowledge of this skeleton until the sinkhole appeared. This is another matter where you'd best approach the council."

Unsurprisingly, perhaps, Sebastian had added nothing to Brian's story by the time Lucy reappeared with a tray. On it, a cafetière and two cups rattled. It was a low tech solution compared with Brian's machine, but still produced an enticing aroma.

"I think we've finished, Sebastian," Neil said. "Thank you for your time. Sherry, do you want to help yourself to a coffee and take it through to the kitchen?"

"I'd love to." Sherry filled a cup and let Lucy lead her from the study, Neil trailing in their wake.

The kitchen was at the rear of the basement, a much lighter room with a door to the back garden. There were no strong colours here. The walls were painted plain white.

"How about something to eat?" Lucy asked. "I could make you a turkey sandwich and a plate of bubble and squeak? There are plenty of Christmas leftovers." Her tone was effusive, bordering on desperation.

While tempted after thirty-six hours of vegan food, Neil was deterred by the wild edge to her voice. "No, thank you. Sherry has some questions about Christmas Eve. I'll take notes." He set up his laptop on the pale wood dining table.

85

"Yes, do tell me about it." Sherry took her cue, sitting beside him and setting down her coffee next to the laptop.

Lucy jumped forward, picking up Sherry's cup and placing a coaster underneath. "Sorry, I should have given you one before." Her eyes flicked between the two detectives, as if waiting to be rebuked.

"No problem. The last thing I want to do is spoil your lovely furniture." Sherry's tone was kind. "You were saying?"

Lucy wrung her hands. She took a seat at the other end of the table. "I thought it was an earthquake. I mean, the ground literally shook and the old sycamore fell over. If it had gone the other way, this house wouldn't be here anymore. The noise was deafening, too."

"You must have been terrified. What did you do?"

"I was scared," Lucy admitted. "But I wanted to make sure Mum was okay. She was in her wheelchair, covered in dust. Dad and I cleaned her up and then he had to check the house." She leaned forward. "I think the carol singing caused it."

Neil silently commended Sherry on keeping a straight face. He speculated about Lucy's mental health.

"Why do you say that?" Sherry asked.

"When we got to the 'Twelve Days of Christmas', we did the actions. All of us jumped up and down together, pretending to be ten lords a-leaping."

Sherry seemed lost for words.

Inwardly, Neil groaned. One of the carollers had been SuperTed. He kept the conversation flowing. "You're suggesting a group of people jumping about caused the sinkhole to appear?"

Lucy hesitated. "Nobody intended any trouble. They didn't know that old cellar was there."

"But you did?" Neil asked. Her cagy body language rang alarm bells.

She twisted a lock of hair around her finger. "I'd heard stories about it."

He pressed on, forgetting his informal arrangement with Sherry. "Have you ever been into that cellar?"

"No. We don't use... We can't get to it."

Neil wasn't convinced. "We'd like a quick look at the cellar underneath this house. I understand the door's locked. Do you know where the key is?"

"No." Lucy fidgeted.

She suddenly seemed much younger. Neil wondered if she had learning difficulties. He would have expected her father to speak up if so.

"Thank you, Lucy. Sherry, any more questions?" He began typing notes again.

Sherry put her elbows on the table. "You've been very helpful, Lucy. I assume you saw the skeleton too?"

"Yes."

"What can you tell me about it?"

Lucy made fists of her hands, resting her chin on them. "It was horrible. Beyond creepy. I can't imagine how it got there."

"We'll do our best to find out. Is there anything else you think we should know?"

"Not really."

"That's all for today, then. Neil will email you a statement to approve." Sherry gave Lucy her card. "Here are my contact details. If something occurs to you, even if you just find the key to your cellar, please get in touch. Phone me any time, okay?"

"Yes. Thank you." Lucy's eyes darted between them, and then down to the tiled floor.

"We'll show ourselves out," Neil said. "I assume the front door on this level is blocked for a reason?"

"Yes. We don't use it."

"Well, thanks," Sherry said. "Goodbye now. Don't forget to call if you remember some detail, however small."

"I will." Lucy stayed seated, twisting her knees and ankles together. Neil felt her gaze on him as he left the room.

They did not see Sebastian again, although Sherry insisted on returning to the sitting room to say farewell to Jennifer. Outside, Neil was relieved to see the press had claimed a further victim. He and Sherry crept away as the cameras focused on a figure beneath an umbrella.

"There's a network of tunnels that was used for French prisoners of war," he heard. One of the women who had been chatting to Brian was parroting his tales.

Round the corner in Jackson Road, another TV van was parking in the space previously occupied by the Aston Martin. Nearby, Neil saw the Z-list diva who had been the centre of media attention earlier. She was evidently waiting to speak to a fresh wave of reporters.

"I hear you're from the police," she said, as he pointed his key fob at the Peugeot.

"That's right." Able to see her better, Neil guessed she was close to Jennifer's age. Fine lines showed through the flawless make-up.

She stood tall, her thin, leather-clad legs like two liquorice sticks, and looked him straight in the eye. "Are you going to remove that dead body any time soon?"

Sherry said in a soothing tone, "I'm sorry, but that can only happen when our investigations are complete."

"Well, I trust they won't take long. The last thing I need is gossip about murders in Jackson Crescent. I've just bought my flat with a bridging loan and I'm sure that sort of talk will affect my mortgage offer."

Neil let Sherry continue to make sympathetic noises.

"I'm sorry to hear that." Sherry sounded as if she meant it. "I assure you we're carrying out enquiries."

"Good. I'll ask Ted to get it done as soon as possible."

They had found SuperTed's girlfriend after all. "We'll be as quick as we can," Sherry promised. "This case is our top priority."

"I sincerely hope so." The diva spun around, strutting away on spiked heels. The two DCs had been the attraction rather than the newsmen.

"Interesting," Sherry observed, once they were safely in the car and on their way. "Strong opinions and a pricy haircut. A blunt-cut fringe is hard to get right. She's a high maintenance woman."

Neil exhaled. "Does the Super know what he's letting himself in for?"

"Not our problem."

"What do you think of the other residents of Jackson Crescent?"

Sherry echoed his own thoughts. "Initial views? Brian Parton is the ultimate good neighbour. I wouldn't say he or Sebastian Freeman have more information for us. Lucy Freeman is different."

"She was evasive. Think she's hiding something?"

"From us, and her father. Maybe those bones are a hundred years old. But if they're not, I bet she knows how they got there."

91

CHAPTER 8

LUCY

Sebastian returned the coffee tray to the kitchen. "Er, thanks for making the drinks. Just to let you know, I didn't intend any gender stereotyping when I asked."

It hadn't even crossed Lucy's mind. She was about to tell him, but Sebastian hadn't finished.

"I would have done the same for you, if they'd wanted to speak to you first."

"Don't worry, Dad, I'm always happy to help. After all—"

"After all, you don't have a proper job, so you like to make yourself useful," he interrupted.

Lucy stared at him. "That wasn't what I meant. And I'm Mum's carer, so I have plenty to do."

Sebastian backtracked. "We both appreciate you." His tone was conciliatory.

Lucy wondered if her mother would agree. It was hard to tell, now the cruel disease had robbed Jennifer of the power of speech. This Jennifer, able to whisper a word salad at best, was nicer than the old one who could talk and write. Heat rose to Lucy's cheeks as she recalled stumbling upon her mother's diary. Why did some events stay with you for decades?

The journal had sat innocently on Jennifer's dressing table, a book covered in a sunflower pattern. Twelve-year-old Lucy had been unable to resist. There, repeated in black and white, were the cutting remarks she'd heard every day.

Seeing them written down made them harder to ignore. 'Lipstick on a pig' was the comment that hurt most. Jennifer had written that it was pointless to clothe Lucy in pretty dresses. The school fees were a waste of money and she didn't understand Sebastian's insistence on treating both children equally. Jennifer's son had sailed through the entrance exam for Bristol Grammar School, destined for a bright future. Her daughter was ugly and fat, even lacking Sebastian's saving grace of intellect.

Lucy tried to stop the memories dragging her back to a dark place. Surely Sebastian was right? Her mother's love had been tough, that was all.

Sebastian broke the evil spell. "What did the police ask you? I hope you said nothing about the cellar."

It had been hard not to, when it was all that interested the two detectives. "I told them about the 'Twelve Days of Christmas', and the ten lords a-leaping. We all did it three times."

"Yes, yes," Sebastian grimaced with impatience. "What about the access? I said there wasn't any."

Lucy gawped at him. "But there used to be," she protested. "Daniel practised there."

Dr Sweet had used the cellar as their rehearsal space and chill-out zone almost every day. Jason had even slept there when he couldn't find a bed anywhere else. She'd brought him food, which served the twin purposes of reducing her calories and giving her an excuse to see him. Typically for Jason, he had been excessively grateful. Lucy was the love of his life, he had declared. She shouldn't have started to believe him. It had been wishful thinking, hadn't it?

"It's twenty years since Daniel set foot in the place," Sebastian said. "The police don't need to know he rehearsed there. I can't afford a bill from the council for repairs to the sinkhole. It would bankrupt me. I'd have to sell this house, if I could get anything for it, that is."

Was that really all that bothered him? She wondered if he knew more about the body than he admitted. The notion was absurd, though. Her father wasn't a murderer. Nor was anyone else she knew.

Sebastian persisted. "You know I made Daniel stop using the space. Your mother said it wasn't safe. Daniel blocked off the passageway, remember?"

That much was true. Daniel had wanted a Halloween party there, and Jennifer had been all for it, until she backtracked suddenly. Might the skeleton have been a Halloween trick? Surely, if it was a plastic toy, the police would have worked that out.

Lucy didn't realise she'd spoken her thoughts aloud until Sebastian replied.

"Of course it's real. There's probably an ancient grave next to the cellar. Occam's razor, if you will."

"Sorry?"

"The simple solution is usually the right answer," he explained kindly. "I can't believe you, Daniel or your mother would have failed to notice a skeleton if you'd seen one."

He must be right. The sinkhole appeared to be in the same place as the vault that Dr Sweet had used for jamming, but she couldn't know for certain. Below ground, without houses and trees and sky for triangulation, the direction of passages was obscure.

She should have remembered that the network of cavities below the Jackson Crescent garden was both confusing and extensive. No-one knew why it existed. She'd never been daring enough to explore it all, but Daniel had. Her older, bolder brother had seen every chamber and tunnel, telling Lucy stories of rats and spiders as big as a cat.

Even now, a grown woman who battled fearsome monsters online, she wouldn't have ventured into the crescent's hidden vaults. Gaming just let her pretend to be brave. Her brother was the real thing.

She and Daniel had thought their very own secret cellar was cool, a fun hangout. Lucy recalled the gloomy air thick with cannabis smoke when his band relaxed. She shuddered at the thought of a dead body nearby. All along, a ghost had been watching them. That cellar had hosted the worst time of her life, but how had she never realised it was an unhappy place until now?

CHAPTER 9

LUCY

Glad to get Jennifer settled in her wing chair, Lucy rearranged cushions to support her mother's back. Jennifer's sitting room was blissfully quiet. In the front of the house, where she slept, a constant hubbub disturbed the peace. Keeping the heavy drapes closed wasn't enough. The thin glass of centuries-old windows couldn't mask the noise outside.

For three days, a stream of trippers and journalists had gathered on the path between number 13 and the taped-off garden. The police were there too. A couple of CSIs worked in the tent, while a harassed police community support officer guarded the gate.

"Why don't you watch the news, while I get you something to eat?" The smoked salmon left from Christmas could be chopped and added to scrambled egg. Jennifer would enjoy a taste of luxury, a pleasant change from the porridge she was usually spoon-fed for breakfast.

Ignoring the lack of response, Lucy pointed the remote control at a picture on the wall. It was a framed vista of sea, sand, and palm trees, chosen by Sebastian. Perhaps he hoped to remind Jennifer of their early married life in Singapore or the expensive holidays they intended to have once Lucy left home.

Those plans hadn't materialised. Lucy had returned from university within a year, her mental and physical health fragile. Sebastian had flatly refused to leave her by herself. Then, as she got better, her dependence on her parents had flipped around. At first, she had helped Jennifer with filing and diary management. It was a salaried position: Jennifer had persuaded her employer to pay. Her job had become too onerous, she explained, and she needed a part-time clerk. Lucy hadn't enjoyed office work, but the wages were fair and it was a chance to help her mother. No-one knew that Jennifer's inability to carry out these tasks herself was the start of a degenerative condition. As the years passed, both women's lives had changed in ways Lucy couldn't have imagined.

The exotic landscape on the wall transformed itself into a television screen. Lucy recognised the local news presenter, a silver fox whose daughter had been in the year above her at school. She now acted with the Royal Shakespeare Company. It was, after all, that kind of school. While not as academic as Daniel's, it attracted parents who paid sizeable fees in the expectation of success. Somehow, with Lucy, it had all gone wrong.

"That was the latest on the travellers in Fishponds," the broadcaster said. "Now we go to Jackson Crescent in Clifton, where our correspondent has bumped into a very famous visitor."

Lucy caught her breath as the screen cut straight to the facade of number 13. Reporters jostled to thrust microphones in a man's face. He flicked a stray curl of black hair out of the brown eyes that had melted a million hearts. His tanned face, fixed on the camera, was smiling.

"It's great to be back in Bristol," her brother announced.

The camera cut to a newsman. "Dan Freeman has flown in from Dubai to support his family."

"That's right." Daniel looked more serious now, his voice concerned. "They're understandably horrified by the discovery of a body nearby. I ask you to respect their privacy."

"Of course." The interviewer oozed sincerity, despite the media encampment outside Jennifer's window. "Are you shocked at a skeleton showing up near your family home?"

Daniel's gaze never left the camera. Lucy felt as if he was making eye contact with her. No doubt all the other TV viewers thought the same.

"I am bewildered and saddened," he said. "Clifton always seemed a very safe place to me when I was growing up here."

"Do you think the death can be linked to Dr Sweet?"

Lucy stared at the screen, her heart pounding. She barely heard Daniel's reply.

"No. I'm baffled by the question, quite honestly."

The journalist tried again. "Mr Freeman, you can't deny there's been a long-running mystery associated with the band. Jason Jardine disappeared, what, twenty years ago?"

"It's nineteen years, two months, three weeks, and four days since I last saw Jason. We were in France." The regret in Daniel's voice was palpable. "Believe me, I have thought about him every day since. I still remember the horror with which I learned he'd left his stuff in the dunes at

Dunkirk. Could I have stopped him, said, or done something differently? It chews at my mind constantly. I can only hope that he's alive and well, and one day he will return."

"What was he running from? Did he have something to hide?"

"If you're insinuating that he killed someone, then no, that wasn't the Jason I knew." Daniel's eyes hardened. "You'll have to excuse me. I came here to see my family."

"But—"

The doorbell rang. Lucy heard a deep voice announce off camera, so loud that it echoed like a faulty stereo speaker, "Mr Freeman has given his interview. He has nothing more to say."

She patted Jennifer's arm. "I'll be back soon."

The letterbox rattled. Daniel hissed through it, "For God's sake, sis, let me in!"

She opened the door. Daniel stumbled inside, followed swiftly by two large, thick-set men. They all wore dark clothing, but of a very different kind. Whereas her brother's garments were designer casuals, his companions looked like bouncers in their cheap suits.

"Daniel! Thank goodness you're back." Lucy enveloped him in a hug.

"Did you hear all that? The guy thinks he's the next Jeremy Paxman." Daniel embraced her, kissing each cheek. The cloying smell of whisky wafted on his breath. "Don't mind Jeff and Steve. They're my security detail."

The chunky men were silent, their eyes watchful.

"What's this about the cellar, sis? I found out on social media for God's sake. You should have phoned me."

"You were busy. I didn't want to bother you."

Daniel tutted. "Just look at that media circus outside. I could have told you that would happen. Are Mum and Dad okay?"

"They're fine." She paused. "Well, Mum's as fine as she ever is. She's stuck in the house now. If Dad or I want to go out, we sneak downstairs, through the back and the garage. He's already left for the day. He went into the uni for peace and quiet."

"I guess his pesky students are on vacation. His favourite time of year. Where's Mum?"

He ought to know she'd be somewhere on the ground floor. "In her sitting room."

"I'll go see her."

One of the heavies said, "Got any coffee?"

Daniel frowned. "Manners, Jeff."

"Sorry, Dan. Please." Jeff's craggy features took on an air of supplication.

"That's better. We'll make a sweet talker out of you yet."

"I'll do drinks for us all. Is it still black coffee for you, Daniel?"

"As the night."

"Strong, milk and two sugars for me and Steve," Jeff said, adding, "Please, love."

The letterbox flap opened, and a slim microphone emerged through the slot. "Can we just—," a disembodied voice said before Jeff shoved the device back outside.

"Please leave Mr Freeman alone now," Jeff bellowed. In a softer tone, he asked, "Have you got a cushion, love? To keep it shut."

Lucy fetched one from the sitting room.

"You can always rely on my sister," Daniel said, as Jeff stuffed the cushion against the letterbox, holding it in place by leaning back against it.

Lucy made her way downstairs to the kitchen, wondering whether Daniel was the only person who trusted her. The thought nagged her as she prepared drinks. She left tea bags to steep in a mug for herself and a sipping cup for Jennifer. Daniel would have the finest Monsoon Malabar beans, freshly ground. It was wasted on the minders but her brother deserved the best.

Rather than take the cafetière up the steps, she waited for the coffee to brew. Outside, a scrawny squirrel wandered disconsolately through the garden. On impulse, Lucy removed a bowl of left-over Christmas pudding from the fridge. Opening the French doors, she scattered a few fruity crumbs on the lawn.

The animal watched from a safe distance, beady eyes sparkling. Once Lucy was back in the kitchen, doors firmly closed, it scampered across to the morsels. It stood there for a while, feeding itself daintily, gaze fixed on hers. She sensed a moment of camaraderie pass between them.

"Enjoy," Lucy said, fully aware the squirrel wouldn't hear. She pressed the plunger into the cafetière, poured coffee into three mugs and added milk and sugar to all drinks except Daniel's. There was extra sugar for Jennifer, to ease her hunger before breakfast. Lucy didn't want to prepare the meal and feed it to her mother, spoon by spoon, in front of Daniel's entourage. Maybe she should phone Sebastian and suggest he came back from work. He could catch up with Daniel in the study and Jennifer would have privacy to eat.

When she returned upstairs with the tray, the heavies were alone in the hall.

Jeff, still defending the letterbox, sniffed his mug appreciatively. "Nice cuppa, ta."

"Better than the plane," Steve said.

"Didn't you travel by private jet?"

"Yeah, from Dubai. Five hours with a broken Nespresso machine." Steve shuddered.

Lucy took the other drinks into Jennifer's sitting room. "Mum, coffee for you and our visitors."

Daniel knelt by their mother's side, whispering into her ear. He broke off from his monologue, stood and stretched. "Thanks so much, sis." He reached for his mug, eyes narrowing as they took in the sipping cup.

Lucy felt obliged to explain. "It's easier for Mum." She placed the tray on a low table by her mother's chair, then tried a mouthful of tea. It was tepid, so Jennifer's would be safe to drink. Lucy held the spout to her mother's lips.

Jennifer managed half of it. Meanwhile, Daniel kept up a stream of anecdotes about his adventures in Dubai. His contract had required him to perform sets on the beach, in the desert and on a superyacht.

"Not bad for a boy from Bristol," he concluded, draining his mug. "Well, it's been great seeing you, Mum."

"You're not staying?" Lucy asked.

"Things to do. I'm on a tight schedule with the next album." Daniel shook his head. "Torch songs, would you believe? My fans are all middle-aged mums now. They don't want music about my wild past. The record company say I should milk my youthful good looks before they disappear."

He was well-preserved. There were no grey strands in his raven-black hair and his skin looked remarkably fresh. How much was down to artifice? Until she'd started painting Jennifer's face, Lucy had paid no attention to cosmetics. Now she peered at her brother's unlined forehead, suspecting Botox and a touch of concealer.

Daniel caught her glance. "Their words, not mine." He replaced his mug on the tray and kissed Jennifer's cheek. "See you soon, Mum."

Jennifer grunted.

"Love you too, Mum," Daniel said.

Lucy followed him into the hall. "Are you sure you have to go? You'll miss Dad."

"I'll see him next time. Can you let us out round the back?"

"Please," Jeff muttered.

Daniel laughed. "Fair play."

Lucy led them downstairs, through the kitchen, and into the back garden. The squirrel had vanished, leaving the square of grass looking lifeless and sad. She shivered in the moist winter air. "You'll have to leave via the garage."

"Guys, can you go ahead and ring the driver. Tell him to be discreet," Daniel commanded, explaining to Lucy, "I sent the limo out of the crescent. It'd be mobbed otherwise."

Lucy unlocked the garage at the rear of the garden. The building usually accommodated Sebastian's SUV and a couple of bicycles, with room to spare. Its sister at number 12 had been converted into a mews house. Today, there was even more space.

"No Chelsea tractor?" Daniel asked.

"Dad took it to work. He's only a fair weather cyclist."

The minders slipped out to Jackson Road, leaving Daniel with Lucy.

"Mum's in a bad way," he said. "She can't even speak."

"She hasn't for years." Perhaps her deterioration was more noticeable because he so rarely visited.

"Do you think she's worried about the sinkhole, the skeleton, and the police?"

"No," Lucy lied. In truth, she couldn't be sure what Jennifer thought. She didn't see any point in upsetting her brother, though.

"Good." He seemed relieved. "Look after Mum, won't you?"

His lips brushed her cheek.

A nondescript black Mercedes hurtled down Jackson Road, stopping in front of them. Jeff jumped forward to hold a door open for Daniel. Both heavies followed him inside while the peak-capped chauffeur revved his engine.

Lucy hastily locked the garage again, hearing the car speed away, returning Daniel to his magical life among the stars. In his childhood home, all that remained of his presence was an empty mug.

CHAPTER 10

NEIL

The small living room was unnaturally spotless. Its laminate floor had been buffed clean, crusty bits removed from the leather furniture, and cobwebs swept away. It hadn't even been this tidy for the landlord's inspection a month ago. Neil lounged on the sofa next to Kieran, savouring his plate of beans on toast. He was glad he'd been at Bridewell all day and had missed out on domestic duties. Of course, Rob and Kieran were more motivated: they hoped to bring girls back later.

"Nice." Kieran finished his food, placing his plate on the coffee table rather than the floor.

"My special recipe. With added chilli sauce." Rob emerged from the kitchen with a six-pack of Foster's lager. He peeled off a can and threw it to Neil. "Catch."

Neil passed it to Kieran. "Not for me, mate."

Rob scowled. "You pussy. We've got to have pre-drinks, right? You need a mortgage for booze at that club."

"Good point," Neil conceded. "I'll have one now, then stick to water later. I'm driving, remember?"

"Suit yourself." Rob lobbed him another can, then flung himself onto the beanbag in front of the TV. In true whoopee cushion style, the sudden compression of air produced a flatulent sound. "Pardon. Must be the beans."

Kieran swigged his lager. "How come you have to drive, mate? Saves us getting an Uber, I suppose."

"I'm taking the car over to my folks tomorrow. Can't afford to get wasted."

"It's New Year's Eve. Live a little," Kieran protested.

"I won't risk losing my job. If I'm still over the limit tomorrow—"

"Yada, yada, yada. Heard it all before."

Neil fell silent. These conversations were becoming too frequent. He didn't gel with his friends as he had in their university days, but he couldn't afford to rent in Bristol on his own. If Gemma hadn't been determined to cool their relationship, he would have suggested they move in together.

Of course, he could find out where the traffic units would be active tomorrow, but that wasn't the point. He was paying a fortune for his car and he wasn't about to crash it. Anyway, he had to drive to Abingdon, so he'd be at the mercy of Wiltshire and Thames Valley police as well. He'd just have to make himself useful and do the washing up while the other lads finished the six-pack.

Kieran and Rob were grateful for the lift to the club, a converted warehouse near the railway station.

"I'll get the beers in." Rob pointed to the neon-lit bar. "Go on, Neil. You can manage one."

"No thanks."

Rob, a regular, got served quickly. He brought Neil a bottle of water. "Can you keep an eye on the beers? Kieran and I are off to the gents."

"Be careful," Neil cautioned. "Remember George."

Rob's face contorted with disgust. "Oof. That's a low blow. Listen, it's party time, mate. Life goes on."

Neil watched them walk through the crowd. Rob's reaction proved his suspicions were justified. His buddies intended to take pills, heedless of their old friend's drug-related death a few years before. How often had they risked their lives for a quick high? He didn't want to know.

He scanned the dance floor, his gaze immediately drawn to three attractive blondes. They wore skimpy tops, miniskirts, and, incongruously, Doc Marten boots. One of the girls whispered to another, who waved in his direction. It was Sherry.

He pointed to the beers on the tall circular table beside him. "I'm looking after these," he mouthed. "What brings you here?"

"Looking after these," she mouthed back, pointing to her companions. "Sisters."

The lads returned, Kieran stretching his legs. He'd drawn the short straw and sat in the rear of the coupé. "Still stiff. I'll be forced to dance," he began to gripe.

Rob caught sight of Sherry staring at them. He nudged Neil in the ribs. "Quick work, dude."

"One each – perfect," Kieran said, aches and pains forgotten.

"Not so fast. That's Sherry and her sisters."

"You dog." Kieran leered, gulping down his beer. "We'll take all three home."

"You'll be lucky." Neil groaned, lips tightening as Kieran swaggered towards the young women.

"You okay?" Rob's expression, curious at first, settled into resignation. "You've changed, dude. You never chill anymore."

"I don't want to be involved. It'll be a car crash."

"We'll find out later, won't we?" Rob followed Kieran.

Sherry stepped away from the group, placing a hand on Neil's arm. "What's up? You're not enjoying yourself."

"I'm staying sober. Driving, you know? And trying to protect your sisters' virtue from my rampant flatmates."

Sherry grinned. "They can protect themselves – if they want to. Kieran and Rob seem nice enough. Want to dance?"

"Why not?" After all, she knew he wasn't on the pull.

She dazzled on the dance floor in every way, and he suddenly realised he was enjoying himself. Before he knew it, they were counting down to midnight and hugging each other, along with their friends and any number of random strangers.

"That was great." Sherry high-fived him. "If you'll excuse me now, I'll resume my search for Mr Right."

"Here?" Neil scanned the cavernous space. "You've got more chance of finding Jason Jardine."

"At least it would make my mum happy." She motioned to the mass of revellers. "Isn't that sweet? My sisters have taken a shine to your mates."

JANUARY 2020

CHAPTER 11

NEIL

New Year's Day dawned early and hangover-free. There was no noise from the household as Neil wolfed down toast and instant coffee, before closing the front door gently behind him.

He'd left the club shortly after midnight in the end. Rob had taken him aside and said he expected to hire a cab; the Peugeot wasn't roomy enough for extra passengers. Later, Neil's sleep was disturbed by his flatmates' voices and the sound of girlish giggles. Whether these were Sherry's sisters or other female company, he had no idea. He hardly gave it a thought as he headed east on the M4 from Bristol. With the dawn light glaring into his eyes, he needed to concentrate on the road.

His tension eased when he left the motorway. No longer half-blinded by the sun, he drove north through the Oxfordshire countryside.

He'd lived in Bristol long enough for nostalgia to hit him on the outskirts of Abingdon. This was the town where he'd enjoyed a happy, secure childhood. A wave of pleasure warmed him at the sight of his family home, a square detached house made of brown brick. An oblong bay sat under a gable, while a garage, too small for a modern car, perched at the side. It was almost identical to its eleven neighbours in the cul-de-sac.

Unlike the residents of Jackson Crescent, his mother did not believe in competitive wreaths. An artificial silver Christmas tree was placed in the lower bay window each year to strike a festive note. This had now been joined by three reindeer in the front garden. Each the size of a large dog, they were constructed of a wicker framework threaded with fairy lights. Two of the deer locked antlers, as if no-one had explained the season of goodwill to them. The third had been positioned to munch on his mother's prized black hellebores.

There was no need to ring the bell. The door opened as soon as Neil pulled into the block-paved drive. His mother stood before him in a sparkly jumper and jeans, Lucas at her ankles.

"Deers fighting," Neil's little brother exclaimed with pride, running out of the house and pointing to them.

"He insisted," their mother said, scooping Lucas into her arms and pecking Neil's cheek. "Lovely to see you. No Gemma?"

"She's had to stay behind to help her parents." It was a lie – their B&B was still closed – but he doubted his mother would Google it to check.

"What a shame. We're all longing to meet her."

"You already did when you stayed at her B&B."

His mother laughed. "Yes, but asking for more coffee hardly counts as a conversation, does it? I didn't know she was your girlfriend, either."

That was understandable. When his family had booked the guesthouse to attend a distant cousin's wedding nearby, Gemma had been a stranger. It was only when he bailed out of the boring reception and went drinking in Glastonbury that she'd become something more. She'd waved to him as he ordered cider at the Riflemans Arms. He'd bought her one too.

"I thought I recognised you," Gemma had said. "You weren't impressed by the soya milk at breakfast."

"I'm sorry I said a naughty word."

"No worries. I could tell you were okay. Not like your Uncle Roy. He's a dickhead."

Neil had to agree. Roy had proved it conclusively by throwing up over the Peugeot on his return from the party. Gemma had helped clean it.

She was a keeper. He would have loved to show her off to his family today.

"There's a misty look in your eyes," his mother said.

Neil changed the subject. "Lucas is talking very well, isn't he?"

"Just like you did at eighteen months. He's besotted with Thomas the Tank Engine, too."

Lucas tugged at his jumper to show Neil. "Thomas Tankshun."

"Engine," his mother corrected him.

"Want to show me your trains?" Neil asked. He had a dim recollection of playing with such things as a boy.

"Choo choo," Lucas said happily, leading Neil inside and upstairs. As the toddler scampered into his tiny back bedroom, Neil was reminded that much had, in fact, changed. This had once been his own domain, but now there was a cot bed, a mobile hanging from the ceiling, and an alphabet frieze on the wall. A cheap train set dominated the floor.

"Choo choo," Lucas repeated, handing Neil a toy locomotive. It was black with a stern face on the front. The tough plastic looked indestructible.

"Great. That'll go fast." Neil hoped he sounded encouraging.

"Mine better." Lucas chose a smilier train identical to the one on his jumper. He guided it around the track.

Neil set his own vehicle on a collision course with his brother's, reversing at the last minute. If there was a competition, he'd let Lucas win. As a child himself, Neil would have given no quarter. His perspective had altered as he grew up. Doing the right thing could be more important than winning.

The biggest shift in his thinking had been accepting Lucas's very existence. The baby's arrival had been a surprise to everyone, not least Neil's parents. Thankfully, they'd been able to stay put. The girls were still at home, but this room was available following Neil's move to Bristol. His father made such good money on the oil rigs that his mother didn't need to work anymore. That suited her fine.

Chuckling devilishly, the toddler made his train accelerate, forcing Neil's off the track.

"Want to watch TV?" Neil asked hopefully.

"Ess." Lucas turned from devil to angel, a cherubic grin creasing his face. He held up his arms to be carried.

Neil took him downstairs, seating him on the leather sofa. It was a larger version of the one in Bedminster, showing how wipe-clean surfaces worked both for infants and young men who had too much to drink.

Their mother found a Peppa Pig programme for Lucas to watch. "Your dad and sisters should be back soon," she said. "Let's have a coffee."

He followed her to the kitchen, watching her start the Nespresso machine and place mince pies in the microwave.

She smiled, her gaze both fond and bursting with anticipation. "Now you can tell me all your news. Working hard?"

The microwave pinged, an aroma of brandied fruit wafting through the air as she took out the warmed pies. She cut the tops open and slipped a spoonful of cream in each. "Here. You were saying…"

"Crime never stops. Even in Bristol."

"Even in Jackson Crescent. I heard about the skeleton. Is it one of your cases?"

"I can't comment." He bit into his pie, nearly burning his tongue on the filling. It tasted good, though.

"Careful. Have a drink of water." She ran the tap and handed him a glass. "About Jackson Crescent. I suppose you remembered it from when you were small?"

"I don't think so." Still, he'd had that strange feeling of familiarity. "When did I go there as a child?"

"I took you with me to a conference at Bristol University. You were four years old. I ran an online bookshop at the time – you know, selling academic texts? My childminder let me down on the day. Anyway, that's how we ended up in Jackson Crescent. I bought some books from Jennifer Freeman—"

"Hang on. Did you say Jennifer Freeman?" Neil knew that, with those words, he'd told her he was on the case.

"Is she still there?"

"You know I can't—"

"—comment," his mother finished drily. "I can, however. She seemed perfect. Too perfect. Actually, she was a typical saleswoman, that's all. Jennifer was very friendly at the conference, then she took me to her lovely big house for a cup of tea. She had a teenage daughter called Lucy, and it was agreed that Lucy would babysit you. Then I could go to the conference dinner."

That didn't sound unreasonable, although Neil couldn't picture Jennifer as a go-getting salesperson despite her framed awards. He couldn't visualise shifty, nervous Lucy as a babysitter, either. Maybe his mother was going to tell him that. "What was the girl like?"

The warmth had left her eyes. Her tone was hard. She replied, "Lucy gave you drugs."

CHAPTER 12

NEIL

"Boss, could I have a word?"

"Not now, Neil. I'm on my way to see Ted Carter. A development in the Jackson Crescent case." Ab looked ready to sprint through the open plan office. He barely glanced at Neil.

"I wanted to talk about that, boss. It's important." Neil had hoped to catch Ab at the gym earlier, but the DCI hadn't showed up. From the bags under Ab's eyes, it was likely the baby had disturbed his sleep again.

Ab sighed. "All right, hit me with it." He didn't break his stride.

"Not here, boss, please. Somewhere private."

Ab pointed to an empty meeting room. "Can you make it quick?" He drew a finger across his throat.

Neil followed Ab inside and shut the door. He blurted out, "I've got intel on Lucy Freeman. My mum says she babysat for me when I was four. And gave me drugs."

"Whoa. Do you remember any of this?"

"No."

Did he, though? His mind clutched at fragments. He'd been spinning around under a big tree, taller than a block of flats. Then he was mixing chocolate icing to make a cake taste better, eating it and laughing. Were these real memories or just fantasies emerging from his mother's revelations? He shook his head.

"Talk me through it as quickly as you can, please. I can't keep Ted waiting."

Neil took a deep breath. "Well, Mum had me young. They didn't have much money then. My dad was still retraining. So Mum had to work, and she couldn't afford proper childcare. She was running an online bookshop selling academic texts, and she had to go to a conference in Bristol. I went with her. Apparently, I behaved well."

"I'd expect no less." Ab grinned.

"Mum met Jennifer Freeman there. Jennifer was very smart and energetic, a saleswoman for a university publisher."

"That would be Lucy Freeman's mother, who you were told had health issues? You didn't interview her."

"That's right, boss. She's almost paralysed and can't speak."

"You did your best," Ab said. "Carry on."

"Jennifer fawned all over Mum. I suppose it was a big sales order, and she wanted to be the new best friend. She took Mum and me back to Jackson Crescent. They decided that I would stay there and Lucy would babysit for me. The two women went out partying together at a conference bash. I was left to Lucy's tender mercies."

Ab raised an eyebrow. "And?"

"As soon as she returned to Jennifer's house, Mum knew something was wrong. I was dizzy, lying on the kitchen floor with my eyes rolling. My pupils were dilated. Mum asked Lucy outright if I'd got hold of drugs."

"And Lucy admitted it?"

"Of course not. She said we'd been eating chocolate brownies. Then she giggled hysterically, over and over. She wouldn't stop. Jennifer threw a wobbler and yelled at Mum for making baseless accusations."

"Okay. Presumably, your mother called the police?"

"No."

"Odd." Ab took a step towards the door. "Did she say why not?"

"Lucy was only thirteen, and Mum thought she'd be in trouble for leaving me with her.

Jennifer had apparently said there would be an adult in the house – her son, Dan Freeman – but there was no trace of him. You'll be aware that Professor Sebastian Freeman lives at the same address. I asked Mum if he was around. She didn't see him either. Thinks Jennifer mentioned a husband working away."

"Right. So there's no independent corroboration of her story. Did your mother seek medical attention? An ambulance, for example?"

"Mum made me vomit, with Jennifer's help, then drink a lot of water. I was okay – no lasting effects."

"You were lucky," Ab said. "So were the Freemans and your mother if her account is true."

"My mum wouldn't lie." Neil reddened.

"No, but she could be mistaken."

"I think Lucy fed me hash brownies. Mum said my mouth and hands were smeared with chocolate. The kitchen was covered in icing sugar and sticky marks. Jennifer had a screaming fit at her precious Lucy for the mess and she said Lucy wasn't allowed cake. That's an extreme reaction, unless she suspected Lucy had laced the food with something."

"Or perhaps she was just angry about a dirty kitchen and children getting over-excited." Ab placed a hand on the door. "I'll discuss it with the Super. It's a potential conflict of interest, as I'm sure you realise. A shame. We may have to take you off the case just as it starts to get interesting."

"What do you mean?"

"It's a murder enquiry now. I've just had results through from forensics. Our skeleton was a male, aged seventeen to twenty-five. The young man was stabbed in the heart. It's amazing what you can tell from little nicks on the bones. They've lain there for around twenty years, so well within living memory. It makes you think someone in Jackson Crescent will know something."

Neil gaped at the DCI, adrenaline surging through him. "I'd really like to help out on this one, boss. Look, I don't even remember spending time with Lucy Freeman as a kid. It won't affect my approach to her as a witness." After all, he was already aware Lucy couldn't be trusted. His mother had merely confirmed it.

"I know. I have every confidence in your professionalism." Ab opened the door. "Unfortunately, it's not my decision."

CHAPTER 13

NEIL

Christmas decorations were long gone and parties a distant memory. Devoid of cheery tinsel, Bridewell once again betrayed its origins as a soulless office block. The MCIT had allocated an incident room to the Jackson Crescent skeleton, and a name: Operation Indigo. The room, a square white box, didn't even have a window to the outside world. A rectangle of frosted glass punctuated one of the internal walls. In late January, little sunshine filtered through from the rest of the building. Harsh fluorescent light overcompensated for it. Another wall carried a flat screen monitor, which Ab used as a virtual whiteboard. He liked his gadgets.

Ab didn't do stress, but Neil thought he looked increasingly worn. No young men had been reported missing in Clifton twenty years ago, but the team had expected house to house enquiries in Jackson Crescent to bear fruit. They were out of luck. Long-term home owners like the Partons and Freemans were rare. Most of the grand houses were divided into flats for aspirational young professionals. Upon starting families, they moved to suburbs where space was more affordable. The crescent's residents were polite, chatty, and produced good coffee, but they denied all knowledge of the dead youth.

DNA matching was taking forever, too, despite pressure from Ted Carter. It was an open secret that the Super's girlfriend was badgering him to solve the murder. As Senior Investigating Officer, Ab bore the brunt of Ted's frustration. On the plus side, Ted had loosened the purse strings. He was throwing resources at the investigation and had agreed Neil should stay on the case.

They needed a breakthrough. Neil was relieved when Ab hinted at good news after their morning gym session. Annoyingly, Ab wouldn't tell the whole story. "We've got the Indigo DNA results," was all the DCI would say, first glancing around to make sure they weren't overheard.

That didn't mean they knew who the killer was. Still, if they had the victim's identity, it was a start.

Neil had high hopes when they both arrived at the incident room. Half a dozen others had beaten them to it. He sat next to Sherry.

Ab's dark eyes flicked around the team, as if mentally taking a register. Finally, he smiled. "Who's heard the latest?"

It was a rhetorical question. Ab continued, "We've got ID on Op Indigo at last. We're as sure as we can be that the skeleton found in Clifton on Christmas Eve was a man called Jason Jardine, and that he died from a stab wound. Straight through the heart, from the position of notches on the ribcage."

Sherry paled. "Boss, is that Jason Jardine, as in Dr Sweet?"

"As in the tragic Dr Sweet, as some segments of the media call them," Ab agreed. "Or the cursed Dr Sweet, because Jason wasn't the only band member to die."

The DCI had done his homework, Neil thought.

"So Jason Jardine is on the DNA database?" Sherry asked.

"I wish life was so easy. Despite rumours that 'Getting High' was written wholly by Jason Jardine, and from personal experience at that, he didn't have a criminal record. We tried the DNA database and didn't get a hit. So we had the time and expense of familial DNA matching."

"Mason Jardine. A dealer in Class A drugs, sentenced to ten years last March." Dave Smeeth, a sergeant in his early forties, was like a walking criminal encyclopaedia.

"Right. Jason's younger brother, who many of you know. I hear he went off the rails after Jason's death. Once we got a partial match with his DNA, we called for Jason's dental records. Bingo." Ab paused. "It goes without saying that this is a very high profile case. We were already fast-tracking it because of the resources used in securing the site—"

And the presence of SuperTed's girlfriend nearby, Neil thought.

"—but now we know Jackson Crescent is the resting place of moody, mysterious, missing Jason Jardine, media interest will be sky-high."

"Jackson Crescent was crawling with cameras on Boxing Day," Neil said. "Including Sky's."

The joke fell so flat that Ab completely ignored it. "Expect more of theirs, and everyone's. There will be a press conference later, but I'm waiting until Dorset police have informed the next of kin. That's Jason's father. He lives in Poole, hence I've asked our colleagues in Dorset to break the news. We should hear from them any time now.

Meanwhile, I'll run through what we know about Jason and his disappearance."

"He vanished in France," Sherry interjected.

"So everyone thought. You have a French degree, don't you, Sherry? Would you like to contact the gendarmes later?"

It wasn't really a question, although Sherry replied. "Sure. But it'll be the French police rather than the gendarmes, boss."

"You can explain the difference afterwards. Meanwhile, a quick snapshot of Jason Jardine. He was twenty-two years old when he disappeared on the third of October 2000. He was a former Bristol Grammar School pupil who dropped out to start a band, Dr Sweet. They didn't make the charts until he'd gone. As far as we know, he'd been couch-surfing and dealing drugs to get by. That's intel. We don't have any actual proof, you understand. The last anyone saw of him, allegedly, was in France. Let's watch a news report from that time."

Dave Smeeth typed on his laptop keyboard. The screen on the wall began to glow.

"YouTube," Dave said. He added a few more keystrokes.

A presenter's head filled the screen. "We're going to Dunkirk in France, known to many for its role in World War Two, and now the scene of a modern mystery."

The camera cut to an aerial shot of a wide, golden beach. Gentle waves lapped at one edge, while the other was bounded by dunes. Zooming in, the camera focused on a pair of Nike trainers laid next to a pile of clothes neatly folded on the sand. Neil saw jeans and what looked like a black formal jacket. A dark grey trilby hat sat on top at a jaunty angle.

"This is a reconstruction," the unseen reporter said, "of what French police found yesterday on this beach, above the high water mark. The clothes, wallet and other items were identified as belonging to Jason Jardine of Britpop band Dr Sweet."

A photograph of the band flashed up, then footage of a concert. The four youths on stage all appeared to be having the time of their lives. The camera lingered on the bass player's excited grin. He was thinner, shorter and darker-skinned than the others. His ginger frizz peeped out from a trilby.

"That's him, right?" Neil whispered to Sherry. "Small guy, mixed race?"

"Got it in one," Sherry told him. "The brains behind the band and their best songwriter, according to my mum. Although she said Dan was lush."

Uncharacteristically, Ab glared at them. They were silent as the news story moved on to an interview with bandmate Dan Freeman.

"What happened?" the reporter asked, still off camera.

"We were about to scout out tour venues in France. We'd just arrived, after travelling through the Chunnel in my Mini." The young Dan Freeman stood on the beach, flicking windswept black hair out of his eyes. His face was classically handsome, from his broad forehead to his chiselled jaw. It was easy to see how he had become the housewives' favourite.

"So, a road trip?"

"Right. But Jason was interested in history, so he wanted to stop for the night in Dunkirk. We checked into our hotel, and he went out for a walk on the beach." Dan Freeman's tone was deep and aristocratic.

"You didn't go with him?"

"I was exhausted from the drive. I crashed out in the room. When I woke up, it was dark, and he wasn't back."

"Did you panic?"

"Not right away." Dan laughed. "I thought he'd found a girl to hang out with. It wasn't unusual."

"When did you realise something was amiss?"

"The next morning. We had to check out by ten, and he still hadn't returned. I went to the police, and they told me what they'd found." He wiped a tear from his eye. "All his stuff…here on the beach. And no sign of him."

"How are you feeling?"

"Devastated. I only hope that he, that he just…" Dan appeared to break down. He barely pushed out the words. "I hope he just wanted space. That he'll be back."

"Thank you. We all hope so too."

Then it was back to the studio, with the presenter asking viewers to call in if they knew where Jason Jardine was.

Dave closed down the screen.

Ab looked up from his smartphone. "Latest info from Dorset police is that they've told Jardine Senior. He is upset, naturally. We'll get a full report later, but the key takeaway is that he's been

135

warned we'll make the news public. So, we can get on with organising a press conference.

"Let's allocate some actions now. Neil, I want you to do a desk review of the misper investigations done at this end nineteen years ago. If any. Sherry is to contact the French police." He emphasised the last word. "Dave, get back in touch with the press office, and get a slot as soon as possible."

"Boss, shouldn't we be interviewing Sebastian and Lucy Freeman again?" Neil asked. "Whatever they say, the body was effectively found in their house. And they must have known Jason, as he was Dan Freeman's friend."

Ab nodded. "It had crossed my mind, and I agree, it makes sense for you and Sherry to go back. And see Dan. But do that background research first. Fail to prepare means prepare to fail, right?"

As Ab allocated tasks to the rest of the team, Neil thought longingly of a large Americano. He nudged Sherry and wriggled his left hand in a drinking motion once Ab turned his gaze elsewhere.

"How are you getting on?" Neil asked Sherry when he brought their coffees back.

"Better than I expected. When I phoned the commissariat at Dunkirk, I had the luck to speak to someone who'd been involved in the original investigation. They said it had been thorough and Dan Freeman was very helpful. That's as much as I learned, though." She sighed. "Speaking French only gets you so far. Now I've got to make a request through the proper channels."

"Interesting that Jason Jardine was a dealer. I bet he sold Lucy hash for her brownies."

Sherry laughed. "The naughty brownies she gave you? Allegedly."

Neil frowned. The team had all heard the story. He'd hoped Sherry would keep an open mind despite Ab's scepticism. "Whatever. She had to get the dope somehow, and Jason's the most likely candidate. Sorry if it shatters your mum's illusions about him."

"Too right. My mum will be horrified if her idol sold drugs to Lucy. Worse, if he gave them to her for services rendered."

"She was thirteen."

"We can't exclude the possibility. It stinks, though, doesn't it?" Sherry wrinkled her nose.

"But suppose instead that Jason was actually a decent guy and not into drugs at all? Ab calls it intelligence, but that's a fancy name for rumours. Mason Jardine, on the other hand, does deal drugs. We know that for definite. That's why he's serving a ten-year stretch. Suppose he sold her the gear and had a bust-up with Jason over it?"

"Perhaps." Neil frowned. "Why would Jason Jardine come back to Jackson Crescent to have a fight with his brother, though? In fact, how would Jason get back from France without a passport or money?"

Sherry rolled her eyes. "To be fair, he could have returned without a valid passport. Travelled via Ireland, or got hold of a fake one. Criminals don't sweat over borders. Jason didn't get caught, but we know he operated outside the law. I bet he had money to get what he needed."

"No bets. Let's establish some more facts and then decide, shall we?" Ab, coffee in hand, lounged against Sherry's desk.

"Sorry, boss. Just chewing the fat." Neil remembered his own drink and took a swig. That first taste was always the best.

"Let me give you the latest news from Dorset. It's poignant. Losing Jason certainly had an

138

impact on the Jardine family, and not in a good way."

"I'm all ears." Neil tugged one for emphasis.

"So, you're right that Mason is a loose cannon. When our Dorset colleagues visited the father, he thought they were coming round about Mason. Makes you think. Although the guy is inside, he's still capable of criminal activity. There's no smoke without fire, is there?"

Sherry nodded.

"The picture they paint of Jardine Senior is a broken man. He used to have a little building business in Bristol. Nothing fancy, but it made enough for him to send his sons to Bristol Grammar. You can imagine the school fees he was paying. He had high hopes for them. When Jason dropped out to play in the band, he threw the youth out of his house. Wouldn't give him a penny."

"The lad started dealing drugs to survive?" Sherry asked.

"Maybe. Won't be the first, won't be the last." Ab's face was solemn. "Jason's mother died of a broken heart when her boy disappeared, as Mr Jardine put it. He blamed himself. Then the younger one got addicted to heroin. Mr J decided

139

he'd made a dreadful mistake cutting off Jason, and he wasn't going to do it again. He closed down his business and took Mason to live in a village in the middle of nowhere. His intention was to get the boy clean. It didn't work."

"Really sad," Sherry said.

"Very. By all accounts, Mr J is drinking himself to death. Anyway, how are you doing? Anything I ought to know before I see SuperTed at the top of the hour?"

"Here's a fact. Sherry's mum has a signed photo of Dan Freeman and Jason Jardine from their heyday." Neil watched Sherry flush.

"Has she, now? Why not bring it in?"

"It's decorating the loo," Sherry protested.

"I'm sure you can persuade your mum to lend it out for a day. Well, if you've got nothing else yet, I'll see you later." Ab hurried off.

With a grimace to Sherry, Neil settled at his desk and began calling up files from the missing person's investigation nineteen years before. Dan Freeman and Jason Jardine had unquestionably left the UK together in Freeman's Mini. Dan had collected a speeding ticket on the way. A snapshot from the road camera captured the car. It was an old-fashioned model, tiny and bright red. There were two faces in the front, Dan squinting at the sun in his eyes, while Jason's signature trilby was pulled down over his forehead.

Two hours later, the car had arrived at the Chunnel. The Customs officer who had checked passports was another Dr Sweet fan. She had been given a photo of the band. Both lads had signed it for her. Neil glanced briefly at the scanned copy, with Jason's neat, rounded signature and Dan's more florid scrawl. He moved on to read reports received from the French police. Maybe Sherry wouldn't need to fast-track the red tape for their co-operation.

She was sitting opposite him, head down at her laptop. He threw a paper plane at her.

"What's this? Don't tell me; it's a party invitation."

"Not quite. There's a lot of useful information in the case files, including reports from France. We can be sure Jason arrived there with Dan, but only Dan went back."

Sherry yawned. "So it confirms what we already know."

"Want to take a look, anyway?"

She sidled around to his desk, picking up his mouse. "Let's see. Oops, I didn't mean to click on that."

It was the scanned photograph. She peered at it.

"You've noticed something?"

"It's all wrong. That signature is different."

"How do you mean?"

"I wasn't joking about Mum having the autographs framed in the downstairs loo. She really is a fangirl. I've seen that picture thousands of times. Dan's name is written out like that: all loops and curls. But Jason's isn't the same. It's an illegible squiggle. We're always teasing Mum it could be anybody's."

If asked, Neil would have claimed he never experienced intuition. At that moment, however, it felt like a blaze of light had illuminated his brain. "There's another photo. I'll show you."

He retrieved the mouse and brought the speed camera snapshot onto his screen. "Who do you think they are?"

"Well, that's dashing Dan. But the guy in the hat—"

"—could be anybody," he finished. "It's not the best quality image, but it's interesting. I was trying to work out how Jason Jardine got back from France. Maybe he didn't go there at all."

"We'd better tell Ab."

They called him over. Arms folded, the DCI listened gravely. When they had finished, he nodded. "Great job. I'm pulling the plug on the press conference. It's time we talked to the frontman of the tragic Dr Sweet."

CHAPTER 14

NEIL

Neil had envisaged Dan Freeman living in a penthouse flat by the Thames in London. He was disconcerted to be driving to suburban Richmond instead. On the capital's western fringes, it was still in the Metropolitan Police area, and Sherry had told them a witness would be interviewed on their patch.

The Met weren't especially interested, despite Dan Freeman's glamour. London had enough murders to keep them busy. They wished Avon and Somerset the best of luck.

As his car drew to a halt in a private road, Neil began to understand what had drawn Dan here. Huge plots hosted mansions adorned with half-timbering, turrets and stonework. One garden alone could have swallowed his entire street in Bedminster. "Dan has privacy, doesn't he? Imagine the parties."

Sherry agreed. "No nosy neighbours. He's free to do what he wants: cocaine, wild sex, murder."

"Better stick to the facts—"

"—as Ab would say," she finished.

Dan's property was a two-storey gabled house. The similarity to Neil's family home stopped there. This was a white-painted, black-beamed, lead-windowed mansion in the arts and crafts style. Although a triple-sized detached garage sat beside it, a bright red Ferrari 488 Spider graced the gravelled drive. A heavy wrought iron gate and railings protected the property. Through them, Neil saw a velvety green lawn in front of the building, and the tops of tall trees behind it. According to maps, the land backed onto Richmond Park.

The sun was low in the sky, gilding the slick, moist grass glimpsed through the rails. Dewdrops glittered: melted frost, which would doubtless refreeze again tonight. Sherry shivered. Although wearing a warm wool coat, she was showing off her legs in black opaque tights and long boots. With her laptop in one hand, she resembled a businesswoman.

"May I?" An excited expression on her face, she pressed the buzzer next to the gate.

A male voice emerged from a loudspeaker, London accent clearly audible. "Yes?"

Neil thrust his warrant card at the remote camera. "Detective Constable Neil Slater. I'd like to see Daniel Freeman, please."

"Can you come back later? He's in bed."

"I'd be grateful if you'd wake Mr Freeman up and ask him to see us," Neil said.

"I'll do my best. Who's that with you? Security, you know?"

"Does he think I'd bring a mass murderer with me?" Neil hissed to Sherry.

She smiled sweetly at the camera and showed her card. "Detective Constable Sheridan Duffy. Sherry."

Her charm often broke down barriers. This time it didn't. With a yawn and a click, the speaker fell silent.

"Dan could be doing a runner round the back. He might even summon a helicopter." Sherry slapped her own wrist. "I should have insisted on help from the Met."

"Let me check the lie of the land." Neil opened Google Maps on his phone. "Look, I can get to the rear of the property. It's just through the park."

The gate suddenly swivelled inwards. Beyond the long expanse of lawn, an imposing oak front door opened. A heavy-set man, bullet head growing like a pale tree out of his dark suit, towered over the threshold.

"Mr Freeman will see you shortly. He asks that you wait inside."

Gravel paths edged the grass and split it into four quadrants. Golden light danced on a sundial in the centre. Feet crunching over stones, the DCs approached the house.

The thug stood with his arms folded, smirking as he ushered them inside. "Don't expect much sense out of Mr Freeman. He was at a party in London last night. Much booze was drunk."

"It was in 'The Sun' this morning," Sherry whispered.

"You read 'The Sun'?" Neil asked.

"My dad likes it," she said, her expression deadpan.

Even more than the houses of Jackson Crescent, Dan Freeman's home displayed his wealth. While the minder loomed ominously by the door, the DCs were told to sit in a room large enough for three chesterfield sofas. A log fire blazed in a carved stone fireplace. Sinking into a denim-coloured velvet couch, Sherry gratefully extended her legs towards the flames.

Jennifer Freeman had chosen showy décor. Her son evidently had different tastes. His sitting room, a harmony of mellow blues and browns, wasn't flash. It simply oozed quality. Neil's gaze was drawn to a full-size beer fridge. Beside it, a drinks cabinet boasted more bottles than the average cocktail bar. They could have been visiting an upper crust club, albeit one where Persian rugs would be rolled back for dancing on the polished floor.

A door opened opposite. Dan Freeman had arrived, looking remarkably well for a man with a hangover. A curl of dark hair fell forward on his tanned, boyish face.

"Good morning. Neil and Sheridan is it? No need to get up; we don't stand on ceremony round here." He perched on a footstool by the fire, then waved dismissively to his sidekick. "Jeff, get us some coffees, then make yourself scarce."

Once Jeff had left, Dan stretched out designer jean-clad legs. He yawned. "Do excuse me. I'm afraid I'm not at my best this morning."

"You were at a film premiere last night with Sadia Safira, I understand," Sherry said.

"Yes, and it's all over the media today." Dan grinned cheerfully. "Sadia may be somewhere nearby. I can't possibly comment. Would you like a whisky? I'm having one."

Neil looked regretfully at the drinks cabinet. "No thanks, coffee's more my scene in the morning."

"I understand. No drinking on duty." Dan pressed a crystal glass into an ice dispenser concealed on the side of the fridge. He poured himself a huge slug of Laphroaig. "If you'd had a wild night like mine, you'd be desperate for a scotch on the rocks. It's crazy. I need pills to get off to sleep and whisky to wake up."

"What kind of pills?" Neil aimed to keep his tone casual.

Dan remained affable. "The kind my doctor prescribes. I've never touched the illegal sort. Anyway, you surely didn't come to see me about sleeping tablets?"

"Definitely not." Neil wondered why Dan had mentioned it at all. "We're visiting in connection with the death of Jason Jardine."

Dan recoiled, almost spilling his drink. "Did you say 'death'? I hoped against hope that Jason was alive. Tell me I misheard you." There was a tremor in his voice.

"I'm afraid not."

"I appreciate how distressing this must be for you," Sherry said. "Neil has some questions, but would you like a few moments to collect yourself first? I need to switch on my laptop to take notes, anyway."

Jeff entered the room again, carrying a silver tray. The white china crockery rattled on it. He was no butler.

Dan stood up straight, obviously trying to regain his composure. He gestured to a low table. "Put it over there and get out." When the underling had left, he said, "Jeff is too nosy. He'll sell all my secrets to the papers one day. Help yourselves."

Sherry immediately filled cups for herself and Neil. "How do you take it, Dan?"

"Not for me, thanks. My God. So Jason's body washed up after all these years?" He sat down, head in his hands.

"Not exactly. His body has been found in Jackson Crescent, Bristol." Neil studied the other man's face. If Dan was a liar, he was a good one. A tear had escaped his dark eyes. Dan swiftly brushed it away.

"Jackson Crescent? That's where I—" Dan's words trailed off.

"Yes. You grew up there, I believe. Is that right?"

"Yes, and my parents and my sister still live there. My God. They might be in danger. Do you know who did it?"

"No. That's why we're here, in the hope you'll remember something that will help us find out. To set your mind at rest, there's no evidence of a serial killer on the loose. Jason Jardine died at around the time he disappeared. His body was discovered in a cellar."

A realisation seemed to dawn, like a light passing across Dan's features. "Ah. You think Jason is the skeleton in the sinkhole?"

"Indeed."

"I'm sure you've made a mistake. Forgive me, I don't mean to be rude, but that's impossible. Jason vanished in France, on the other side of the English Channel."

Sherry interjected gently, "It's no mistake. We have incontrovertible DNA evidence. I'm sorry, Dan."

Dan rubbed tears from his eyes again. "I guess I was clutching at straws. But it's so hard to believe. Absolutely earth-shattering. I can't really assist you, either. The last time I saw Jason was in

Dunkirk. In fact, I spent a great deal of time with the French police trying to find him."

"Don't be so sure you can't help. Cast your mind back nineteen years, and tell me why you set off for France." Neil stifled a shudder. He must have been to Jackson Crescent himself at around that time. Luckily for him, he'd only eaten drugged cakes rather than ended up dead in a cellar. How many more heaps of bones would they find if they inspected the vaults properly? It might be months before they could do so, unfortunately. The police couldn't explore further until the council made the sinkhole safe. He had told Dan there was no serial killer to worry about, but who really knew?

Dan took a deep breath. "We were scouting tour venues. The band operated like a collective. We didn't have a manager. Our first single charted in Europe before the UK, and we thought we'd capitalise on that. I had a list of contacts in Paris, northern France, and the low countries. They were all interested, but we needed to suss out these places. I volunteered because I could parler français. Also, I wasn't tied up in a day job like Gaz and Pete."

"Did anyone go with you?" Neil thought it did no harm to play dumb occasionally.

One of Dan's eyebrows twitched. "Well, Jason, obviously."

"Did he speak French too?"

"No. Hands up." Still holding his glass, Dan mimed the action. "To be frank, he volunteered because my mother gave me cash to stay in hotels. It meant we'd get beds to sleep in and three square meals a day. Jason didn't always have that. He was basically homeless."

Neil moved on to asking Dan to describe the journey, from the start in Bristol until the moment Jason left their hotel room. Two decades later, Dan repeated the contents of the police files. Jason had turned up for breakfast in Jackson Crescent, reluctantly cooked by Jennifer. Dan's mother regarded Jason as a freeloader.

Dan's own behaviour sounded similar, Neil mused. Perhaps it was different when it was your own child.

The two bandmates had driven away in the rusty old Mini, so fast the car had rattled alarmingly.

"All Minis did that above sixty, and we were way over." Dan's shoulders relaxed. He looked almost happy.

"Couldn't your parents afford to buy you a better car?"

"They weren't minted. Lucy's school fees had to be paid for. I'd had various scholarships, but there was no chance of that for her." The odd, jarring note of resentment vanished as Dan grinned roguishly. "I've got better cars now."

Neil allowed himself a split-second of envy. "Carry on. You said you arrived at the Eurotunnel?"

"In Folkestone. Yes. We drove through passport control. Turns out the immigration officer had seen us play at her uni six months before. She was a fan. You can always tell. They light up like a Christmas tree…"

"And she asked for your autograph?"

"Of course not. She was totally professional. I handed her the passports and said, yes, we are with the band. We had a bit of a chit-chat and I asked if she'd like a photo."

"Which you signed there and then?" Neil felt like a coiled spring ready to unwind.

"Yes, we had a box of merch in the boot. Jason chose a nice picture, we made our marks on it and we'd made her day."

154

"We've got a copy of that very photograph." Neil glanced at Sherry.

She removed the printed image from her case, and passed it to Dan.

"Good God," Dan marvelled. "Four young reprobates. Who knew what the future would hold?"

"Are those signatures yours and Jason's?" Sherry asked.

"Without a doubt."

"Then whose are these?" She handed over a photocopy of the picture from her downstairs loo.

Dan stared at it. "Mine, naturally. The other looks like Gaz's. He signed it in the wrong place, I guess. We used to get a load ready in advance before our gigs. Look, I've got boxes of them stashed away with other Dr Sweet memorabilia. It's my pension plan in case my career goes tits up." He looked smug. Clearly, he didn't think it likely.

"Can you dig some out now?" Neil asked. "With Jason's signature, please."

"No problem." Dan rose to his feet. "It'll take a few minutes. Want more coffee?"

"Please." Sherry rarely refused an offer like that.

Moments after Dan left the room, Jeff brought another pot.

"Thanks." Sherry smiled at him.

Jeff merely grunted before disappearing again.

"Chatty, isn't he?" Neil poured coffee into their cups. "What do you think of Dan's reaction to the photo?"

"Plausible," Sherry said. "I'd reserve judgement until we've seen more."

Dan returned with half a dozen black and white snapshots. He spread them out on the table. "See, here's the full set. Me, Jason, Gaz and Pete."

At first glance, Jason's neat autograph mirrored the signature provided at Folkestone. Disappointment tugged at Neil. He kept his face impassive. "Mind if we take these?" he asked, more in hope than expectation.

"Go ahead. I'd like them back, please." Dan gathered them together and handed them to Neil.

"I've got one more picture to show you. This was taken by a road traffic camera." Sherry produced the print.

Dan chuckled. "Ha. Me and Jason in the Mini. I remember that speeding ticket. Bang to rights, I'm afraid."

"Are you sure it's him?" Neil asked.

The musician answered without hesitation. "Absolutely. Look at the way he's avoiding the sun and catching up on his sleep. He had a dreadful hangover." Dan gazed fondly at the grainy image.

Neil continued to quiz Dan about the trip to France, learning nothing that he didn't already know. Dreams of progress dwindling, he moved on to discuss what happened next.

"Any idea why Jason might return to your home, or how he would get into that cellar with no apparent means of access?"

Dan dropped the bombshell that Neil hadn't dared to hope for. "Yes," the musician said.

CHAPTER 15

LUCY

The media were no longer a constant presence in Jackson Crescent, although a grumpy-looking PCSO remained. While the white-suited CSIs had left, their tent had to be guarded from the sightseers who were still very much in evidence. Lucy did her best to ignore them. Playing the piano for Margaret Forsyth and her students was usually the high spot of her week, but she was apprehensive about making her way to Margaret's flat next door. If the garage of number 12 hadn't been converted to a mews house, she might have been able to slip around the back.

In any event, despite averting her gaze from every living soul, Lucy bumped into a young man on her way out of number 13. She didn't recall seeing him before. He had a studious air, and at first she imagined he must be one of the brainier teenagers who walked from the crescent to Bristol Grammar School each morning. Daniel had been among them once.

He peered at her through trendy spectacles. "Lucy Freeman? I'm with South West News

Online. What do you think of the latest developments in the sinkhole murder?"

She gawped at him, unsure what he meant.

"I understand the police have made an identification," he pressed. "I assume you've heard?"

"No." It hadn't been mentioned on TV earlier. She added, "Who is it?"

"I rather hoped you could tell me."

"Sorry, I can't."

He was still blocking her passage. Lucy glanced around for a means of escape. Her eyes lit on Brian further down the cobbled path, spreading tourist misinformation. He waved to her.

"There are smugglers' caves underneath the garden," she heard him say. "It's a honeycomb of tunnels, and one leads to the church. The vicar used to store brandy in the crypt. He moved it here when the excise men were on their way. The smugglers had an insider—"

"I think you should speak to Brian Parton over there," she suggested to the reporter, ignoring a twinge of guilt. Brian was equal to the challenge. In his view, journalists and sightseers believed anything. He enjoyed testing them with improbable stories.

She pressed the buzzer for Margaret Forsyth's flat, a duplex occupying the basement and most of the ground floor of number 12. Nobody came, although Sasha began to bark. A phone rang somewhere in the flat. It stopped abruptly and Margaret's patrician voice could be heard answering it.

The dog's clamour grew more insistent. Eventually, Margaret opened the front door, a phone clamped to her ear. Sasha leaped out like a furry bullet, almost tripping up the journalist before scratching and whining at the garden gate.

The PCSO, a rotund man in his forties, bent down to scratch the dog's ears. "It's more than my job's worth to let you in," he said softly. It was the first time Lucy had seen him smile.

Sasha ambled past Brian, accepting cuddles from the day-trippers around him. She found a patch of thistles to water at the side of the path and made her way back to Margaret just as the first student arrived.

This was Bea, a sixth former at Lucy's old school. Thin, dark and pretty, she would have intimidated Lucy as a contemporary. As it was, they tolerated each other.

"A new dog?" Bea stared at Sasha, then Margaret.

"I'm looking after her for my son," Margaret said. "Her name is Sasha, and she's very sweet." She sighed. "I'm sorry, Bea. Unfortunately, I've just had bad news. My daughter has flu and needs help caring for her baby, so I'm going to have to cancel my lessons."

"Oh dear." Bea's smile looked forced.

Margaret softened. "We can have thirty minutes now if you like. I'll waive my charges on this occasion. Then I'm afraid I'll have to start packing and make arrangements for the dog."

"Sasha can't go with you?" Lucy asked.

"Sadly not. My daughter and little Bella live in a fourth-floor flat. There's no lift, no space for a dog, and it's hardly suitable."

Hoping the fee waiver wouldn't stop her being paid, Lucy followed the others inside and sat at Margaret's piano. A polished cream baby grand, it dominated the music room.

Margaret, pausing to pick up a speck of dust from the ivory carpet, took up her customary position in a chair beside the piano. Bea stood in the centre of the room, a music stand in front of her.

"We'll begin with 'Tomorrow Shall Be My Dancing Day'," Margaret announced. "Have you been practising?"

Bea nodded.

"Ready, Lucy?"

Lucy struck the first chord.

Sasha wailed mournfully.

"Wait. The dog cannot carry a tune," Margaret declared. "Let me see if I can distract her." She gave Sasha a toy fashioned from knotted rope.

The Samoyed sank her teeth into the knick-knack, shaking it energetically.

"Simple things," Margaret said. "Now, where were we?"

Lucy began playing again. The dog, blessedly quiet, preoccupied herself with the toy even when Bea began to sing.

Margaret seemed to judge the lesson a success, promising Bea to find her another tutor if the visit to London took more than a week.

"So, Lucy," Margaret said, once Bea had left, "here's ten pounds for your trouble. I wish we had more time to talk. Bea is improving, but her voice will never be a patch on yours."

Lucy stared at the teacher, both relieved to be paid and astonished at Margaret's comment.

Margaret hadn't finished. "Bea works hard, and I have commended her for it, but you have a natural talent. Even your mother, who was somewhat sparing with praise in your younger days, used to say so. Your voice is excellent and you could have done more with it. You achieved Grade 8, did you not?"

Lucy blushed. "That was a long time ago. Anyway, Daniel was always streets ahead." He had received the lion's share of compliments from their mother, which was only natural. It must have been clear to Jennifer that her son was incredibly gifted and her daughter an awkward failure.

"Daniel was ten years older, I believe? Really, Lucy, I know you're very busy, but I think you could spare an evening each week for a choir. I meant to tell you ever since the carols. Your father can look after his wife occasionally, as I presume he's doing at the moment."

"Don't you have to go, Margaret?" Lucy shifted her weight from one foot to another. She didn't want this conversation. Nor did she wish to leave her mother for too long. Sebastian enjoyed amusing Jennifer with anecdotes about his students, or finding audiobooks and TV programmes for her. The basics of life, laboriously cleaning and feeding her, were less to his taste.

"You're right. I must leave soon. Promise me you'll think about it." Margaret turned her gaze to Sasha. "What are we going to do with you? My son wanted to avoid kennels, but you can't legislate for a family emergency."

"I don't suppose anyone in the crescent would have her?" Lucy suggested. "How about Brian and Marilyn?"

"I know, the obvious choice. Sadly not. I'm sure Marilyn is allergic to dogs."

Sasha's brown eyes appealed to Lucy, as if the dog understood too much.

"We could take her, perhaps." Lucy bit her lip. Why had she blurted out those words? She didn't have the authority. Jennifer had said no to more pets after the guinea pig's untimely demise. Her father remembered too; there was no doubt about that. Hadn't he said on Christmas Eve that Lucy couldn't keep an animal alive for more than a fortnight?

She chewed harder, tasting blood. It was unfair to judge her on events that had taken place decades before. Looking back, she still couldn't work out why the two goldfish had died, or how the guinea pig had broken a leg. Daniel had been forced to put it out of its misery.

Struggling to work out how to retract the offer, she stared at Margaret.

Before Lucy could backtrack, Margaret flung her arms around her. "That would be wonderful. Just perfect, in fact. Samoyeds are such sociable animals. There's always going to be someone in your house to keep her company. I'm amazed I didn't think of it before."

It wasn't such a great idea, Lucy thought, desperately. The dog was adorable, and far more communicative than a guinea pig, but Sebastian's objections must be overcome. Who could win an argument with a philosophy professor? "I'll just—"

"Let me gather leads, food, bowls and her other paraphernalia. She likes a walk down the Zig Zag path at precisely 10am and 3pm. You can do that for her, can't you?"

Lucy shuddered. The Zig Zag was a vertiginous path running from Clifton down the side of the Avon Gorge. The journey down to the river wasn't a problem, but returning uphill would be a challenge. Still, she had a head for heights, as would anyone living in a house like number 13. It was basically a staircase with rooms hanging off it.

That was the least of her worries. Sasha, barking with excitement, nudged her. Lucy looked away, unable to make eye contact with either the dog or Margaret. How on earth would she convince her father?

CHAPTER 16

NEIL

"Go on." Neil tried to keep his excitement under wraps.

Dan's eyes were fixed on his. "You could get to that cellar from our house. It wasn't exactly easy, given the hazards involved, but we had the ideal rehearsal space for the band. A huge room with natural soundproofing."

"Hazards?" Neil probed.

"You had to make your way through a tunnel leading from our own cellar. It wasn't full height, so you'd stoop, and there were stalactites and stalagmites. We ran a couple of extension cables for electricity. The other lads tripped over those." Dan grinned. "We didn't care too much about health and safety. A roadie would be appalled."

"Even so, you played music in the old cellar. Who else could have used it?"

"No-one. It's probably not accessible anymore. That tunnel appeared to be on the point of collapse years ago. Mum put her foot down after a while, and said it was too dangerous for us. But all the band kept spare keys. Jason may have left some kit behind. One of his guitars, say. He must have come back to fetch it."

"Talk me through that. You say he had a key. To what, exactly?"

"Our basement. There's a door to the street at that level. Have you visited Jackson Crescent?"

Neil nodded.

"Then you should have seen it. So, he would have come into the basement, walked past Dad's study, then there's a door leading to steps—"

Sherry interrupted. "Did your father know your friends had keys and were using the cellar?"

"Good God, no. He'd be at the uni or globetrotting with his conferences. Mum knew."

"What about Lucy?" Sherry asked.

"Well, obviously Lucy knew. She was always hanging around the band."

That was a field for future enquiry. Neil set it to one side as he picked up the questioning again. "Who had copies of those keys?"

"Me, and everyone else who lived there. So that would be Mum, Dad and Lucy." Dan began counting with his fingers. "Then Jason, Pete and Gaz. They were the guys in the band at that time. And Sarah."

"Who's she?"

"Sarah Stokesley. She was Jason's girlfriend for a bit. A wild child." He laughed, not unkindly.

"How well did Jason get on with each of those individuals?"

"He and I were best mates. We set up the band together. Jason never argued with me, but he did with Gaz and Pete. They thought he did too many drugs. Ironic, isn't it, as Gaz was a smackhead? Live and let live, I say." Almost imperceptibly, the corners of Dan's mouth turned down.

"How badly did they argue?"

Dan finished his whisky. "I'll need another of these if you're going to take that line. I can't believe Gaz and Pete would have hurt a fly." He helped himself to an even larger measure.

"Did Jason have any enemies, so far as you were aware?"

"Not me, Gaz, or Pete. Dr Sweet were like family." He gulped more of the amber liquid. "Mum disliked him, as I mentioned. She thought he was a bad influence. Jason wrote the lyrics to 'Getting High', after all."

"Anyone else?"

Dan stared into the depths of his glass. Finally, he knocked back the contents. "I don't like to say it, but Sarah argued with him constantly. She and

Jason were on and off like a lightbulb. Hell hath no fury, as the Bard said. Then there was Lucy."

Now they were getting somewhere. Adrenaline rising, Neil opened his mouth to ask the killer question about Dan's sister.

Sherry got there first. "An interesting phrase, 'Hell hath no fury'. Why do you say that?"

Neil stiffened. Now, of all times, she had chosen to ignore their informal agreement.

"Sarah wanted him on a string," Dan said, his voice bitter. "She dumped him, but then she decided to take him back. He wasn't having it. I wouldn't be surprised if she murdered him when I was tied up in France, helping police with their enquiries. I always thought he just planned to take time out. He'd got the hassle with Sarah, and life with the band got intense the closer we came to success."

"We'll talk to Sarah," Sherry assured him.

"Do that."

Neil took control again. "You mentioned your sister, Lucy. Can you expand on that?"

"This is really hard for me." Dan sighed. "She had a crush on Jason. Ask anyone in the band; they'll tell you that."

"There aren't many left to ask," Neil observed.

"True. My apologies. A poor choice of language. You could see Pete, who's playing with cars down in Bristol. His first love." Dan stared at his empty glass. "Now, I don't wish to speak ill of my sister, but it was embarrassing. She actually tried to look like Sarah, for God's sake. Dieted herself twig-thin, lightened her hair, copied Sarah's mannerisms. Mum called it attention-seeking behaviour, and I knew exactly whose attention Lucy was after. I'm sure she made a play for Jason after Sarah ditched him. He turned her down. Forcefully."

"Excuse me asking you this," Sherry jumped in again, "but how do you know that's what happened?"

"Jason told me about it."

"So you're sure he said no?" Sherry pressed.

Neil stayed silent. It churned his stomach, but Sherry had a point.

"What do you take me for?" Dan's eyes were cold. "I'd never hang out with the kind of pervert who would touch my little sister." He looked away from the detectives, his gaze settling on the whisky bottle. Nonetheless, he didn't move.

The fire crackled and popped, the woodsmoke-scented air heavy with the weight of unspoken words. Neil said nothing. He knew instinctively that Sherry would do the same. Ab had drummed it into them: let others fill an awkward silence, and you never know what you might hear.

Eventually, Dan spoke. "I would have trusted Jason with my life, but I can't vouch for Lucy. She's always been away with the fairies."

"Can you give me an example?" Neil asked.

"When she was a kid, all her pets died within days. She's so self-centred and irresponsible, she couldn't even look after a goldfish. I'm not saying she was crazy enough to lure Jason to Bristol and keep him captive in a dungeon, but… Well, if she did, it's no wonder he didn't survive."

"We'll talk to her, too," Neil said.

Dan winced. "I hate to think this, but she'd be my prime suspect. What a mess. My best friend dead, and my sister…" He stood up, clearly hoping they would leave. "Please call me any time if further questions occur to you, or even if you'd like to shoot the breeze. Keep me informed, too. I genuinely want to help."

He showed them out himself. Perhaps surly Jeff was taking a tea break.

As Neil negotiated outer London's traffic jams, Sherry seemed lost in thought.

"What do you reckon?" Neil asked. "Good leads?"

"He wore make-up."

Neil snorted. "Really? No wonder his appearance had hardly changed since that ancient video. But what's that got to do with anything?"

"Dan Freeman is a performer, and I think a performance is what we got. I'm going to ask our Dorset friends if they can get an example of Jason's signature from his dad. And I'll tell Ab to be careful. Dan is a seasoned traveller, and he's loaded. He could melt into thin air as fast as you can say 'passport'."

Perhaps, brought up to believe Dan Freeman was a god, she was disappointed to find him less than perfect. Neil couldn't be bothered to ask, nor argue that Dan was a singer, not an actor. "He couldn't have been more helpful. Now we know the cellar can be reached from number 13. And Lucy lied to us about it."

At last, they could give Ab some good news. They had another witness in the form of the bandmate in Bristol, and two suspects, both female. The Sarah Stokesley angle could be interesting. Neil's money, however, was still on Lucy Freeman: a proven liar, pet killer and drug user. He was lucky to have survived in her care as a four-year-old.

CHAPTER 17

LUCY

Sasha stood by the French windows in the kitchen, whining and staring meaningfully at the garden. She barked as soon as Lucy caught her eye.

"All right, I get it. It's time for your walk."

Sasha's barking went up a decibel. The animal skipped around the table and nudged Lucy's hand.

Setting down the dirty plates she was about to place in the dishwasher, Lucy checked the old railway clock on the wall. It was five past ten. Margaret had said Sasha should be taken out at 10am and 3pm precisely. Who knew dogs could tell the time?

"I'll remind Dad we're heading out, okay?"

She didn't have to. Sebastian stood at the threshold to the room.

"I see Sasha is making her feelings known," he said. "Listen, before you go—"

Sasha barrelled into him.

Sebastian kept his balance. He patted the dog's head. "Sit. Good girl."

Immediately, Sasha sat quietly.

"How did you do that?" Lucy asked.

"You've either got it or you haven't. She can sense an alpha male." He might have been joking, but it wasn't clear, especially when his half-smile slipped. "Now, I've got sad news, I'm afraid. Daniel just phoned. The police visited him yesterday. The skeleton in the cellar has been identified as Jason Jardine."

Lucy's mouth fell open. For decades, she'd pictured a lively, laughing musician, strumming tunes on a beach in France. The fantasy crumbled at her father's words. She was unable to speak.

Sebastian misunderstood. "You don't remember him, do you?" he said gently. "Jason was one of the boys in Dr Sweet. The bass player."

"I know." Her legs wobbled. She sat down.

"It's terrible, isn't it? Daniel is distraught."

She imagined he was, but why hadn't he phoned her as well as their father? Daniel knew how much Jason had meant to her. Still, however great her shock, Daniel's must be ten times worse. Jason had been his best friend.

"I'd better ring him," she said.

The dog yipped, seemingly in protest.

"Call him later," Sebastian said. "I told him you'd gone out on the Zig Zag with Sasha because

I thought you'd already left. Anyway, I've comforted him as best I can."

"Are you going to tell Mum?"

Sebastian sighed. "I was about to go upstairs to sit with her when Daniel phoned. Let's not say anything. It would only upset her."

Lucy nodded. She rested her fists on the table, letting it take her weight as she stood. When she moved away to pick up the dog's lead, she found she was shaking. With some difficulty, she clipped it to Sasha's collar. "We'd better go."

"You will be careful out there, won't you?" Sebastian said. "You aren't used to dogs, and that one is a handful."

"I managed last time."

It had been a pleasant surprise when her father had welcomed the animal with open arms. Perhaps he was starting to accept the idea of a pet.

He followed Lucy up to the ground floor. "One more thing," he whispered. "Daniel is sure the police will come back here. Obviously, whatever happened to Jason is nothing to do with you or me. I told them we didn't use the cellar, and I suggest we stick to that story. Saying anything else won't bring Jason back to life, after all, and I don't want trouble from the council. Okay?"

"Understood."

"Good girl." They were the words he'd used to the dog earlier. At least he didn't tell her to sit.

As she enveloped herself in parka, hat and gloves, she heard him ask Jennifer, "How about a podcast on morality this morning?" His voice was unnaturally bright.

There were trippers outside, trying to engage the reluctant PCSO in conversation, but no journalists. Lucy supposed they would arrive again soon. Still trembling, she let the dog lead her away from Jackson Crescent. As Margaret had said, Sasha had a habitual route and knew it. The animal also wanted to move fast, and there was little point in resisting. Samoyeds were sled dogs and strong pullers. Sasha charged round the corner onto Jackson Road and continued at speed. The shock of Jason's death had no chance to settle and work through Lucy's mind, nor did she have time to admire the scenery. She focused on staying upright as the dog dragged her over icy pavements.

They rushed past ice-cream-coloured villas and red stone terraces until the network of streets ended at Christchurch Green. Presided over by a handsome old church, this was an area of parkland dissected by roads and paths. After waiting for a bus to chug past, Sasha crossed the highway sedately and stopped on the green, inclining her head towards the leash.

"You want me to take that off? All right."

The cold, crisp day had transformed the green into a winter wonderland, pale with frost. The snow-white dog was in her element, rolling on the icy grass and snuffling at trees for squirrels.

At last, Lucy had a moment to reflect. She should have known Jason was dead. Although she'd hoped otherwise, it had become an impossible dream as the years stretched past. If he'd been alive, lying low to sort his head out as Daniel put it, he wouldn't have cut all contact forever. Yet he'd last been seen in Dunkirk. It didn't make sense. How come she hadn't twigged he was back in Bristol, in their secret cellar of all places? How had he died there?

Her phone vibrated, and she took it from her pocket, hoping Daniel had texted. Instead, she saw a message from Xander, asking why she hadn't been gaming for a week. Was she okay?

Lucy sent a terse reply, "Sorry. Can't/won't talk," then immediately regretted it and followed with, "Fine but busy". She could hardly blame

Xander for being concerned, but she only had head space for Jason's death right now. Xander should have realised before that she wasn't online as often as she used to be. As Jennifer's health deteriorated, it was becoming physically and mentally demanding to care for her.

A middle-aged woman led a small brown dog along the green from the opposite direction. When their paths crossed, she said, "A Samoyed, if I'm not mistaken. New kid on the block?"

"I'm looking after her for—." Lucy stopped. What was Margaret: a friend, a neighbour, or her boss? Why were people so nosy, anyway? You walked dogs because they needed it, not because you wanted conversations with every stranger who wandered past.

Sasha stopped sniffing animal trails and pranced towards the newcomer, a terrier-like breed. Both wagged their tails.

"Gorgeous girl." The woman stroked Sasha's silky coat.

"Your dog is nice too." Lucy gave in, grasping that she was supposed to reciprocate. "What sort is it?"

"Dido is a 57 varieties."

Lucy tickled Dido's ears. Yesterday, she had enjoyed virtually identical encounters with other dog owners. A few children had stopped to pet the Samoyed. She didn't know any of their names and she hadn't volunteered hers.

Sasha nipped at her lead for attention. "Sorry, I think she's telling me to go." Lucy fastened it to Sasha's collar. They proceeded to the far side of the green, bordered by the road to the Suspension Bridge. Here, Sasha paused. Margaret or her son had evidently done some training.

"Go," Lucy said.

Once they had crossed the road and a tiny patch of grass at the top of Sion Hill, Sasha sped up. Gravity on her side, the dog raced past a long white sweep of grand houses, towing Lucy towards the splendid Avon Gorge Hotel. This was situated at the crest of the gorge, where the road flattened out. Here, the Zig Zag path snaggled down the ravine's edge to the river below.

High above, to the right, Brunel's majestic Clifton Suspension Bridge soared across the Avon, white tracery like lace against the grey clouds. As the dog halted, Lucy had a fleeting recollection of her delight at the view yesterday. Oblivious to Jason's death, she'd been at peace.

For once, she hadn't envied Daniel his jet-setting lifestyle, or even his luck at spending the first ten years of his life in exotic Singapore. He'd told her stories about it throughout her childhood, speaking of sunshine and beaches and palm trees. There were frightening tales of huge spiders, too. Her mother never mentioned those. When Jennifer had spoken of the city state, she'd boasted about her parties and servants. It was clear she'd never wanted to leave.

If Jennifer had got her wish and Sebastian hadn't insisted they return to the UK with Lucy on the way, how different all their lives would have been. The Freemans would never have met Jason and he wouldn't have ventured into a cellar in Jackson Crescent, little knowing it would be his grave. Lucy blinked away tears.

The dog, sensing her distress, licked her hand.

"Ah. I should unclip your lead."

Released, Sasha headed straight for the tarmacked path. The Zig Zag was slippery with frost, but it didn't bother the pet. Sasha ran free, often stopping to inspect the undergrowth nearby. Lucy followed, her steps small and cautious.

A jogger ascended towards them. Lucy worried that the dog would jump up at the woman.

Luckily, Sasha continued to explore a clump of ivy, saving Lucy both from embarrassment and the need to talk to the runner.

Hands in pockets, Lucy walked on ahead, recalling Jason's sweetness, chewing over questions she couldn't answer. She waited, shoulders hunched, where the footpath looped around like a tight boomerang. Stone walls held in the earth above, while railings on the lower edge of the path protected humans and dogs from the precipice beneath. Here and there, the rail was broken. Lucy stared at the drop, wondering what it would be like to fall all the way to the Portway, the busy road running alongside the river. Would it bring a quick end to grief and desire and the feeling of being totally worthless?

Sasha hurtled around the bend, on course to tumble through the gap.

"Slow down!" The words emerged as a scream.

Sasha came to a standstill and gazed soulfully at Lucy.

"Nice dog." Almost crying with relief, Lucy ran her fingers through the fluffy fur. She picked up a twig and threw it towards a safer spot. Here, a rough bench, merely a slab of wood on metal legs, offered respite to walkers. A gnarled old tree behind it served as a barrier to the slope. No-one would brave the seat today: it was thick with frost.

Sasha chased the twig and sat chewing on it, wagging tail thumping the ground. Lucy wished she could share the dog's joy. Even the animal's happiness didn't bring a smile to her face. Sighing, she threw another twig, making sure it landed away from the railings where the dog might slip through. Thus, they continued down the crooked track until they had arrived at the Zig Zag's final stretch, a dizzying set of steps down to the Portway. Here, the gurgle of the rushing river competed with the hum of cars zooming past.

Lucy replaced Sasha's lead.

"Be good," she instructed. A stone wall prevented them both plunging into traffic, but it would be easy to stumble and fall if the dog pulled too hard. Yet, perhaps distracted by a pungent aroma of foxes, the Samoyed dawdled.

At the foot of the steps, Lucy tugged the lead to indicate they would walk on the level ground beside the Portway. Sasha would have none of it. With a merry bark, the dog turned and began climbing back up the steps.

"As you wish," Lucy said. She panted with the effort of following until she realised she could let

Sasha do most of the work. Straining at the leash, the Samoyed pulled Lucy upwards.

At the top of the Zig Zag, Sasha stopped. The dog's face broke into a grin and she licked Lucy's hands.

"You're my friend, aren't you?" Lucy smoothed the fur between Sasha's ears, her heart lightening as the dog returned her adoring gaze.

Sasha wasn't her only friend, of course. Margaret Forsyth seemed to like her, and Xander, although she did nothing to encourage him. People needed her too: Jennifer, and by extension, Sebastian. However pathetic she might be, she had reasons to live.

As if travelling through a mirror, they retraced their steps in reverse. Lucy didn't look back at the Zig Zag as Sasha led her past the hotel, up Sion Hill and across the green. They had been away for no more than thirty minutes, and the dew had already melted.

Sasha had worked out that number 13 was their destination. Outside the house, only the PCSO remained. On impulse, Lucy offered him coffee as he stroked the dog. It turned out that he was kept well-supplied by Brian and Marilyn, with whom he was already on first name terms.

Lucy unlocked the front door and unclipped Sasha's lead. The dog immediately raced into Jennifer's sitting room.

"Good girl. Who's my favourite fluffball?" Sebastian's voice combined with the animal's excited barks.

Lucy followed Sasha. While Jennifer sat peaceably in her wing chair, entertained by headphones, Sebastian lounged on the sofa. One hand held a textbook. The other accepted a series of licks from the dog, in the manner of a Roman emperor receiving tribute.

"How's Mum?"

"I've decided she should refresh her memory on philosophy, and given her Aristotle to listen to. She seems to like it."

Lucy rather thought Jennifer would prefer true crime stories or a chick lit novel. She decided to swap audiobooks once Sebastian's back was turned.

"Going to uni now, Dad?"

"I don't have lectures till this afternoon." He continued to fuss over the dog.

Lucy offered coffee, and was halfway down the stairs to the kitchen when the doorbell rang. She heard paws dashing into the hallway.

"Can you get that?" Sebastian called.

The walk must have worn her out. Puffing at the exertion, Lucy returned to the ground floor and opened the front door. The dog, tail spinning like a furry windmill, waited with her to greet the visitors.

"Hello, Lucy. We've got some news to share with you. May we come in?" Sheridan, the friendly policewoman, beamed at her. The less amiable detective, Neil, glowered silently.

The dog whined for attention until, without waiting for pleasantries, Neil planted a foot inside. Sasha took this as a signal to jump up at him.

"Down," Neil commanded, to no effect.

"She just wants to be stroked," Lucy said, "and lick your face."

"You're kidding," Neil said. "It's a dire wolf, right?"

"As in Game of Thrones?" Lucy stared at him. "Apart from being white and fluffy, Sasha is the least wolf-like dog ever. She loves everybody."

"For breakfast?" the detective asked. His tone was not jocular. Still, he tentatively scratched Sasha's ears. They arrived at a mutual understanding in which he permitted the animal to lick his hands.

Eventually, the dog transferred her affections to Sherry, who had come inside and shut the door.

Neil glared at his wet hands. "Is this your pet?" he asked.

"No, we're looking after her for a friend." The saga was too complicated to explain.

Sebastian marched out of Jennifer's sitting room. "You have information for us, I hear?"

"We have some questions for Lucy," Neil said.

"We like to interview individuals separately, even if they're members of the same household." Sherry flashed an ingratiating smile. "Perhaps we can meet you later in your study?"

The policewoman was beautiful, Lucy thought, realising Sebastian had noticed too.

"No problem," Sebastian said. "I have to get over to the university before one, that's all."

"You'll have plenty of time," she promised. "Now, Lucy, can we speak privately? Please lead the way."

Neil glared at the Samoyed. "Can I wash my hands first? I assume there's a bathroom nearby."

"Over there." Lucy pointed.

She waited with Sherry while Neil washed slobber off his hands. Sebastian had returned to Jennifer's side. Lucy overheard him saying the police had turned up again and she shouldn't worry. He would keep her appraised of developments.

Sherry paid court to the dog. The policewoman seemingly charmed every creature on the earth, and Lucy couldn't even bring herself to be jealous. What was the point? It wasn't as if Lucy never felt plain in comparison to others. A fairy godmother had smiled on Daniel at birth, blessing him with cleverness, talent, and good looks, while his sister made do with the scraps that remained.

There was a stark divide between Neil and Sherry as well. In an alternative universe where she could join the human race, Lucy would have liked Sherry as a friend. By contrast, Neil was grim, spiky, and suspicious. In a computer game, he'd be a dark lord, or perhaps a torturer. The pair epitomised the good cop, bad cop routine. Lucy had previously supposed it existed only on TV or in the pages of novels.

Neil reappeared. He nodded to Lucy, which she interpreted as a request to take the detectives to the kitchen. She obliged.

It was just past eleven o'clock. Lucy suggested coffee. Although Neil accepted, it didn't buy any brownie points with him. He sat, elbows on her

189

kitchen table, frowning as she filled a cafetière and took the best china from a cupboard. The mustard-yellow cups were Wedgwood, decorated with gold leaf. She hoped the detectives would be gentle with them. Jennifer liked this set. At least if a piece got broken, Jennifer wouldn't find out.

Sherry sniffed the air appreciatively. "Thank you. I remember your divine coffee."

"You're welcome." Lucy pressed down the plunger and poured drinks for the two detectives. She chose a seat across the table from them.

Sherry leaned forward. "We've identified the body in the sinkhole. We believe it's an individual known to your family. Does the name Jason Jardine mean anything to you?"

Should she admit that Daniel had told them already? Under Sherry's sympathetic gaze and Neil's cold one, Lucy decided to pretend ignorance. She blushed, silently castigating herself. They would sense something amiss. "Yes," she faltered.

Neil looked like a beast about to rip out her throat. "Can you expand on that?"

"Tell us how you knew him," Sherry said, her tone much softer and matter-of-fact, as if they were just two young women at a coffee morning.

190

"He was in my brother's band." Lucy felt uncomfortably warm now, despite the breeze from the French windows. They didn't fit well. She kept meaning to tackle it. Up in her bedroom, where Jennifer couldn't see, she'd sewn curtains in a Day of the Dead print. There was enough material left over for a fat, sausage-shaped draught excluder. Jennifer wouldn't know about that either, and Sebastian probably wouldn't notice.

"How often did Jason visit this house?" Neil asked.

Lucy wished the detectives would stop this ping-pong game of questions. It would help her focus on one of them when she delivered her answer. "Not very often," she said.

Neil didn't look convinced. "Why did Jason visit?"

"To see Daniel. I mean," she stuttered, "Wh… why would they tell me? They were adults, and I was just a kid."

"It wasn't, perhaps, to rehearse?" The look of disdain on Neil's face seemed to intensify.

"They may have done… sometimes."

"In the garden cellar?" he asked.

She realised that he knew. Of course he did. How stupid of her, imagining she could keep the access route to the cellar a secret. Jason and Gaz would tell no tales now, but the police had spoken to Daniel already. He must have told them, and if he hadn't, Pete or Sarah would have done.

Lucy nodded. "Yes, they used it for rehearsals." She didn't need to say that Jason had slept there or that she'd slipped him unwanted dinners.

"And," Neil said, with the air of a man about to deliver a knife to the jugular, "when did you last see Jason Jardine?"

She dared to peer inside her mind, recalling that final encounter in technicolour detail. The cellar had been lit by bright, fluorescent tubes, the sort you picked up and moved around. Daniel and Jason used to pretend they were light sabres. This time, Daniel hadn't been there. She'd been alone with Jason, drinking in the sight of him: eyes wide and gorgeous, skin perpetually tanned and a smile like sunshine.

How had it all gone so wrong? She shuddered, her cheeks flaming. "It was just before he left for France," she said. "He said goodbye. There was nothing out of the ordinary about it. I didn't know he was going to disappear. I didn't know he was going to die. I didn't know I would never see him again."

Those details were true, but she omitted more. Despite raiding Sebastian's whisky and getting blind-drunk after that fateful meeting, she couldn't obliterate the memory. Wild horses wouldn't drag it from her, though. "I can't tell you anything more," she said.

CHAPTER 18

NEIL

A press conference was scheduled at last, for 11am. According to Ab, SuperTed was receiving earache from his girlfriend. Ab did not expect Sarah Stokesley to tell them anything of significance, but he still wanted Neil and Sherry to reach her before the media storm kicked off again.

Sarah hadn't been hard to track down. She'd left Bristol but hadn't changed her name. Her home was a commune in the Somerset Levels, a place called Beechwood Farm. It sounded idyllic, but Neil was unimpressed by the flat brown fields he passed as he drove Sherry there. The sky, a great leaden bowl, threatened a deluge at any moment.

"Doesn't your Gemma live round here?" Sherry asked.

"Closer to Glastonbury. And she's not 'my' Gemma."

"I'm sorry." Sherry sounded concerned. "Hit a raw nerve, did I?"

It was nearly a month since he'd shared a kiss with Gemma on Boxing Day. Keeping his eyes on the road, he hoped Sherry would take the hint from his silence.

She didn't. "It's tricky with all the overtime lately. Annoying that it's SuperTed's pillow talk that's causing it. You haven't fallen out with Gemma, have you?"

"Not exactly, but she won't move in with me. She likes the countryside too much." He scowled at the dull scenery.

"Show her the sights of Bristol. Invite her to stay for a weekend. Your flatmates are away skiing soon, aren't they?"

"She's not into clubs and cocktail bars."

"Try a walk in the park, then. And get your credit card out." Sherry giggled. "What girl can resist the January sales?"

"They're nearly over."

The road rose through a thicket of twisted trees, entirely bare of leaves and as unappealing as the rest of the landscape.

"That's it, there," Sherry said. "Beechwood Farm."

He had nearly missed the faded and peeling sign. Neil pulled into a rutted driveway in front of the farm's metal gate.

"Want me to open up?" Sherry asked.

"Please."

As she jumped out of the Peugeot, three noisy geese appeared in the farmyard, gathering by the gate.

"Brought bread, Neil?" Sherry asked, barely audible over the cacophony of honking.

"That's for ducks, isn't it?"

Sherry pulled the latch anyway, scattering the birds as she pushed the gate open.

This was the functional underbelly of rural life, not the pretty face that Gemma's parents presented with their B&B. Neil drove into the yard, a stretch of bare earth with a house in front and open barns to each side. One contained a tractor and farm implements, the other a rusted Land Rover and a shiny MG Midget. Neil doubted the latter would get out to the road except in fine weather. He winced at the sight of his Peugeot's tyres pressing down on the soft ground. There would be trouble once the rain began.

Sherry's smart black boots picked up mud, too, but at least they protected her ankles from being pecked. The geese clustered around him, shrieking, as he left the car. He remembered Gemma saying they were used in lieu of guard dogs. At Beechwood, they seemed to be an adjunct. Barking could be heard in the shabby grey stone farmhouse before him.

A short, middle-aged woman appeared at the door, almost dwarfed by the Alsatian at her side. "Lost, are you?"

The geese hadn't attacked but that dog was giving him the evil eye. Neil hung back, flashing his warrant card from a distance. "I'm looking for Sarah Stokesley."

"That would be me. Whatever you want, can you be quick about it? I've got to get packed and get out to market." She stood solidly in the doorway, one hand on the Alsatian's collar. Quiet again, the dog panted, skewering him with its gaze.

Neil squinted at her. Press photographs from twenty years ago showed a waif-like figure with a blonde pixie cut. Even a police mugshot, taken when she was arrested for possessing cannabis, had been hauntingly beautiful. There was nothing left of that Sarah Stokesley. This woman was chunky, greying fair hair tied back, her face broad and weather-beaten. Finally, he realised her eyes were the same: free of coyness or make-up now, but still large and brown.

"Well? Are you planning to stand there all day? I've got work to do."

Sherry strode forward, showing her card too. "May we come inside, please? We have news that may be upsetting."

"You can tell me here."

Sherry, in full-on empathy mode, leaned in towards Sarah. "It's about Jason Jardine. We found his body."

The emotion that flickered across her features vanished so fast that Neil couldn't pin it down.

"What makes you think I care?" she asked, her voice almost a whisper.

"You were close to Mr Jardine once, I understand," Sherry said.

Sarah grimaced. "That was years ago. Before he went to France. That's where you found the body, I suppose? Anyway, I guess you'd better come in. Shut the door behind you." Without waiting for a reply, she turned, still holding the dog.

"He wasn't in France," Sherry said, as Neil closed the heavy oak door.

That shocked Sarah. She stumbled, the dog slipping from her grasp and baring its teeth at the visitors.

"Can you control that dog?" Neil kept his voice neutral. There had been a fleeting look of contempt in Lucy Freeman's expression when he recoiled from her pet. He didn't want to lose face in front of another suspect. Besides, animals could smell fear, couldn't they?

"He won't harm you." Sarah didn't sound particularly convinced.

Neil had received similar assurances from dog owners in the past. An episode from his childhood came to mind, the memory of a Jack Russell trying to bite a finger off. Thankfully, the Alsatian didn't slobber all over him like Lucy Freeman's unruly mutt. He gave it a wide berth.

Sherry stroked the top of its head. "What a lovely dog," she said. "What's your name, poppet?"

"He's called Grimdark," Sarah announced.

"Grimdark. How unusual. There's a good boy." Sherry turned to Sarah. "Is there somewhere private we can sit down?"

"It's all private. The only folk in this house are me and Ethan, and he's in bed. The rest have taken our veg to market. They'll be in Clevedon by now and I should be on my way. So you can come through to the kitchen, but you'll have to stand. There's cakes on all the chairs."

They followed her down a chilly corridor, the smell of vanilla wafting ever closer. Sherry enquired about the baking and received a detailed answer. There were at least ten types of bun, tart, brack or brownie on their way to the market.

Sarah's reply was different when Neil asked what vegetables they cultivated on the farm. Snippily, she told him there were all sorts. He wondered if their crops included marijuana. Although he hadn't caught the scent of it, this was the kind of remote location where it could be grown under the radar. Perhaps he would suggest an investigation to Ab later.

Heat enveloped them as Sarah led them into the kitchen, a beamed chamber with rough stone walls. A huge range cooker warmed the air and perfumed it with sugar and spice. True to Sarah's word, the gaudily painted furniture was covered with towels, on which sat trays of cakes. These weren't the sterile conditions Neil expected from a commercial bakery, but at least everything seemed spotless.

"Don't get too close," Sarah warned them. "It's all hot." She pointed to a stack of cardboard boxes in the corner. "I'll be filling those while we talk, all right? Meanwhile…"

She picked up the dog, lifting it easily despite its bulk, and put it outside the back door. "Best to remove temptation," she explained.

It was clear that no refreshments of any kind would be offered. Neil supposed Sarah might sell him a brownie if he gave her money. He stood at the threshold to the room, watching Sarah busy herself while Sherry did her best to make eye contact.

"Neil will take notes on his laptop," Sherry explained. "Oh dear, there aren't many places he can put it down. How about that shelf? He can stack those saucepans to create a bit of space."

"Okay." Sarah's tone was grudging.

"You'll have the opportunity to review what I've written," Neil offered.

"Sorry, I won't have time."

"We'll email you," Sherry said. "Now, can you tell me about your relationship with Jason Jardine?"

Unexpectedly, the question produced a smile. "He was the love of my life," Sarah said.

"Really? How did you meet?"

"The band played at a schoolfriend's eighteenth. I got chatting to Jason and we hit it off. You may not believe this looking at me now, but I was a straight A student. My dad had high hopes. To say he was upset when I fell pregnant is an understatement. He was beyond strict and out the other side, like Jason's father. Maybe that's what drew us together. And our love of music."

"You're musical too?"

"Of course. Jason and I planned to form a duo together. He stopped writing for Dr Sweet." She looked sharply at Sherry. "You were aware that he wrote all their songs? Forget the statements the band put out, about being a collective. Jason was the only creative one."

Sherry nodded. "There have been rumours about it. In 'The Sun', I think. Anyway, you said you had a side project with Jason. Why didn't that go ahead?"

"It wasn't a side project." Sarah tossed her head. "Jason intended to leave Dr Sweet. We had it all worked out."

Neil heard footsteps on the flagged floor behind him.

"'Scuse me." A tall, thin youth dashed past. He positioned himself between the two women, appealing to Sarah. "Mum?" A lock of dark, wavy hair fell across his face. "I can't get my car to go. Can I have some money for repairs?"

"There isn't any, Ethan. I haven't been to market yet. Use the MG Haynes Manual."

"I did." He had an air of triumph. "It needs new parts. Haven't you got a few quid stashed away?"

"Ask Grandad, please. And can you run up to the attic, and put buckets under the leaks? I'm talking to my visitors."

"Okay." He glanced curiously at the two detectives, his smile dropping. Abruptly, he stalked back out of the room.

Ethan had obviously identified them as police. Neil was even more suspicious about the farm now.

"Kids," Sarah said ruefully, placing flowery china plates in one of the boxes. She added a tea towel as padding. "I don't suppose you have any; you're too young."

"I'm not married yet," Sherry admitted.

"Didn't stop me. Not that Ethan was exactly planned, but I'm glad I've got him now." She began to cut a tray of millionaire's shortbread into squares.

Sherry said, soothingly, "It's good that his grandfather is supportive. I guess Keith Jardine gets a share of Dr Sweet's royalties, even if, by rights, he should have had it all."

Sarah stared at her. "I've no idea what Keith Jardine does. We're not in touch. You couldn't possibly remember, as it's such a long time ago, but he dragged my name through the mud. I had to go into hiding. He gave interviews to all the redtops, blaming me for Jason's suicide in France. I blamed myself too. But you say his body wasn't found in France?"

"It was in England," Neil said, afraid Sherry would give too much away. Once the delayed press conference took place, Sarah would learn Jason had died in Bristol. Until then, they might glean more by keeping the news vague.

Sherry flashed him a warning glance. She evidently had a reason for her disclosure. "When did you last see Jason, Sarah?"

"Two days before he left for France. If he did go to France."

"We believe he did," Sherry said. "Did you discuss the trip at that meeting?"

204

"No. We didn't really talk. I told him I wanted to cool things down. Actually, I was seeing someone else."

Neil blanched. He had been mildly surprised that Sherry seemed certain Jason had travelled abroad. Sarah's reply, however, was like a punch to his gut. Gemma had used similar words to him. She didn't want their romance to grow stronger. Had she found another man?

Sarah filled and packed a dozen Tupperware containers. "I'd never seen Jason so angry before. There was no chance we'd work as a duo after that. He stormed out of my house." She laughed without mirth. "It wasn't my house, of course, but my dad's. I ran away not long after, when he insisted I had an abortion. No way would I do that. Never. It's ironic because he dotes on Ethan now."

"The Grandad who gives him money?" Sherry asked.

"That's right. Cut me off without a dime, but he bought Ethan an MG for his eighteenth birthday. By that age, I was living here. Lucky, really, that the old hippies at Beechwood took me in." The bitterness in her face softened. "This is all Ethan has ever known. I don't make music anymore, but there's always room for a cake maker."

By the looks of her, she'd eaten plenty too, Neil thought.

"I've encouraged Ethan to see my dad," Sarah continued. "Who knows, the boy might learn how to get rich, or…" Her voice trailed off.

"He doesn't seem that wild," Sherry said.

"He's not." Sarah sighed. "I just don't want him to end up like me, working hard without prospects. If it wasn't for Ethan, I'd have completely wasted my life. He's a good kid. Lately, he's even been saying he'll sell his car to pay for the roof. Jason would have done that. I think of Ethan as my little piece of him."

"Isn't he entitled to a share of the royalties then?" Sherry asked.

They could use the money. The roof needed fixing, there was no sign of central heating, and no paint job could disguise the shabbiness of the furniture.

Sarah shook her head. "I approached Keith about that. He said Ethan isn't Jason's son."

"Surely you can get a DNA test done?" Sherry looked incredulous, justifiably so. Sarah didn't seem the kind of woman to be deterred easily.

"I don't want to." Sarah didn't meet Sherry's gaze.

Neil began to understand.

Sherry did too. "You're not sure he's Jason's son, are you?"

"No."

"Dan Freeman's?" Sherry asked.

The question hit Neil out of left field. In his mind, he pictured Dan and Ethan side by side. There was some similarity about their hairlines and the way they carried themselves. He wouldn't have made the connection himself, but he didn't stare at a photo of Dr Sweet every day.

Sarah pursed her lips. "That bastard ruined my life. If I was tied to him by the only person I love, it would be my worst nightmare. And Ethan's. Unless Dan Freeman could find a way to use him, he'd reject Ethan without a second thought. My son shouldn't have to go through that."

Rain began lashing the window. Grimdark whined at the door. Sarah relented and let him in.

"Behave." She waggled a finger at him. The dog slunk into a corner and lay down, sulking.

"Can you explain a bit more about your relationship with Dan Freeman?" Sherry asked.

"There's nothing to tell. Dan seduced me. It was full on: flowers, poetry, promises. After weeks of love bombing, I really thought he cared, and we

had a future together. I broke up with Jason."
Anger fizzed through Sarah. She boxed up the
remaining cakes, working efficiently yet glaring
all the while. "Dan wanted that to happen. Can't
you see that? He didn't want Jason to leave the
band and work with me. But Jason disappeared
instead. A week later, when Dan returned from
France, he dumped me. Said he couldn't stand the
guilt."

That was interesting. Dan Freeman hadn't
mentioned his role in the split. Had Jason even
known about it? Neil was relieved when Sherry
picked up on the point.

"How did Jason take it when you left him for
his best friend?" Sherry asked.

Sarah shrugged. "I didn't tell him it was Dan I
was seeing. If Jason found out, he must have made
his peace with Dan, because they went to France
together."

"Were you aware of friction between them?"
Sherry said.

"No. I know what you're implying." Sarah
looked her in the eye. "If Dan Freeman was on
fire, I wouldn't cross the street to piss on him. But
I'll tell you this. Dan would never have killed
Jason, not over me, nor any other reason. Jason

wrote the songs. He was the goose who laid the golden eggs."

CHAPTER 19

NEIL

Neil returned from the Somerset countryside at lunchtime, stomach rumbling. More actions had been allocated for the day by then. He hardly had time to grab a sandwich before Ab sent him on his way.

"This is a waste of time," Neil complained, as he drove through the fringes of the city centre. "I've told Ab we need to bring in Lucy Freeman for questioning, not interview half of Bristol."

"I'm sure he's on it." Sherry sounded sympathetic. "Pete Willoughby was with the band, though. Like you said to Dan, there's just the two of them left."

Neil turned onto the Feeder Road, a long, straight strip bordered by a canal on one side and functional warehouses on the other. Unlike the prettified stretches of water in Bristol city centre, this was not houseboat territory. It had an unloved, gloomy air about it.

Every cloud had a silver lining, however. "Rob claims there's a good microbrewery around here," Neil said.

"And an excellent bakery. Cakes to die for. Sarah Stokesley's didn't look bad, though. Were you tempted?"

"Was I ever. Wish I'd bought a brownie or two."

He savoured the remembered scent of chocolate and vanilla. It was just chiming with an earlier, dreamy fragment of memory when he found P&F Motors.

The body shop was announced by a sign smaller and even more dilapidated than Beechwood Farm's. Neil edged along a lane bounded by a high wire fence on one side, and cars in various states of disrepair on the other. This gave out onto a tarmacked yard with a workshop, its open shutter revealing yet more vehicles. Tacked onto one side was a Portakabin containing a counter with an office behind.

Neil parked in front of it. Now the press conference was over, he wouldn't have been surprised to see reporters at Pete Willoughby's workplace. Fortunately, the only person around showed every sign of being an employee. A girl in her late teens or early twenties, she sat at a desk in the office. She appeared to be taking selfies.

The morning rain had swept through, leaving puddles behind. Neil and Sherry picked their way past them. He pushed open the hut's door. A blast of warm air welcomed him. There was a faint aroma of boiled sweets.

The girl rose to her stilettoed feet, tiptoeing to the counter. Her clothes suggested a clubber rather than a clerk. She wore a black garment which, made with the minimum of material possible, could barely be described as a dress. Her make-up was heavy too: airbrushed skin and artificially long lashes, framed by a tumble of lilac curls.

"Yes?"

Sherry showed her ID. "We'd like to see Pete Willoughby."

"You mean Dad? He's out salvaging a wreck." Her accent marked her out as Bristolian. Sherry could undoubtedly say which part of the city she hailed from.

A phone on the counter rang, its bell harsh and strident. Willoughby's daughter tutted and picked it up. "P&F Motors?"

There followed a lengthy conversation about engine failure and likely causes. Ms Willoughby became animated. She clearly knew about cars and enjoyed discussing them.

A tow truck pulled up outside, boxing Neil in. The driver entered the office, whistling. "Sorry my lover, delayed in traffic."

Despite his leathery skin and the bags below his eyes, the newcomer was recognisable as Pete Willoughby. He was short, his black hair slicked back just as in the old photos of Dr Sweet.

His daughter pointed to the phone, then the two visitors standing by the counter.

"How can I help you?" Pete sounded as Bristolian as his daughter. If he'd attended the grammar school with Dan Freeman, it hadn't left a trace in his diction. He removed fingerless gloves, muffler and padded jacket. "My life, it's warm in here. Turn down that heater, Rosie."

She glared at him, and wrapped up the telephone conversation with, "That's all booked for you then. Tomorrow, at eight."

Neil took out his ID card. "We're police detectives. DC Neil Slater and Sheridan Duffy."

"Ah. Investigating Jason's murder, are you? I've had the press on the phone already, offering me money."

"You want to be careful what you say to them. This is a live investigation."

"Shouldn't they be careful what they print?" With his hooked nose and alert eyes, Pete reminded Neil of a carrion crow.

"Potentially," Neil admitted. He must make an effort to be less spiky. Pete Willoughby was an important witness.

"Look, Rosie, do you want to sort out that camshaft? I'll mind the office." Pete grinned as the girl picked up an overall and pair of boots from a coatrack, and disappeared behind a door marked WC. "She hates it in here. Just helping out while we're short-handed."

No coffees were offered here, either. Pete swivelled a section of the counter out of the way and led the detectives into his office. It was little more than a cubbyhole, and a tight squeeze for three people. Neil and Sherry sat on moulded plastic chairs, facing Pete across the only desk. This was occupied by a computer with a bulky, old-fashioned monitor, and sheaves of paperwork.

Sherry positioned her laptop on top of an invoice book. "Mind if I take notes?"

"Be my guest, lover. What can I tell you?"

The edge of Neil's chair bit into his buttocks. He shifted slightly, banging his elbow against an adjacent filing cabinet. "We'll wait for your daughter to go outside if that's okay."

Rosie emerged, curls tied back. She inched round the desk, swung the counter to one side, and left the cabin.

"Anyhow," Pete said, "you'll probably want to know when I last saw Jason."

"You read my mind." Despite his discomfort, Neil liked the ex-musician.

"The reporters asked me that." Pete chuckled. "I'm sorry. I know a death is no laughing matter, of course I do. It's so long since I saw Jason, though, it doesn't seem real anymore. It was the day before he went to France with Dan. We had a rehearsal round at Dan's—"

"Where in the house, exactly, was this rehearsal?"

"That cellar that collapsed. I'm sure Dan told you already."

"He did," Neil said.

"Things weren't great between Dan and Jason, what with Dan pinching Jason's girlfriend. You knew about that?"

"Yes," Neil said, "but I wasn't aware that Jason did. How did he find out?"

"Gaz let it slip. A remark to Dan about sloppy seconds, as I recall." Pete winced and nodded to Sherry. "I beg your pardon, my dear. It's lads' talk. He was speaking in jest."

"No problem," Sherry said. "I've heard much worse, as Neil will confirm."

"How did Jason take the news?" Neil asked.

"He had words with Dan. I won't repeat them in front of a lady. Then they both got on with it. To them, the band meant more than any woman. My wife didn't agree with that attitude, incidentally." Pete chortled. "Dan kept his head down, while Gaz and I tried to keep Jason's spirits up. It wasn't really his fault, and he was the mainstay of the band in a way. He wrote all the music, with a few riffs from Gaz."

"I thought the band wrote the songs together," Sherry said.

About to kick her foot, Neil realised she was deliberately playing dumb.

"We were a collective. We all put our names to the songs. Dan insisted," Pete told her.

Neil frowned. "You said things weren't great between Dan and Jason, yet they went to France together?"

"They avoided each other to start with – as much as you can when you're jamming together. Jason said he'd still go to France. Poor lad didn't have much choice. It was the only way he'd be sleeping in a proper bed."

That backed up Dan's account. Neil maintained a poker face. "What were Jason's usual living arrangements?"

"Not good." Pete grimaced. "Jason slept wherever he could. He was homeless, so we all looked out for him. Sometimes he stayed over at Sarah's. He had to be quiet there: her dad would have lynched him if he'd found out. Old Man Stokesley never understood the twentieth century, let alone the twenty-first. Oftentimes, Jason kipped in Dan's cellar. They left a sleeping bag out for him. Then I'd let him shelter in my Transit if he asked. Did they tell you the van was why I joined the band?"

"That hasn't been mentioned."

"I'm not a posh boy like the rest of them, am I? I heard on the grapevine they wanted a drummer with a van. Dr Sweet had a bubbly Britpop sound, and I fancied a piece of that. When I auditioned, they didn't care so much about my drumming. They needed wheels, and they liked mine."

"Why did you leave?"

"Musical differences. Listen, do you mind if I vape?" Pete removed a vape pen from his pocket.

Unlike smoking, it wasn't against the law. At least Pete had asked. "Go ahead," Neil said.

Pete took a drag, exhaling a strawberry-scented cloud. That explained the sweetish smell in the air.

Sherry coughed.

"Sorry." Pete turned his head away on the next breath. "If I'm honest, it all went wrong once Jason vanished. We should have split there and then. But we didn't because Dan found us a new manager."

"Alfie Bucks," Sherry said.

Pete's eyes widened at the unexpected interruption. "Yeah. Big Bucks. How did you know?"

"She's a fan," Neil said.

"I was against it, but I was outvoted. And the Alfster knew his stuff, all right. He milked Jason's disappearance relentlessly. 'Getting High' zoomed up the charts. As did the first album. At last, we hit the big time."

"So you left just as it all started to go right?" Neil observed. "You mentioned musical differences."

Pete laughed without rancour. "The standard answer to a question like that. It's always more complicated. Things weren't going right, not at all. Jason had written crazy, catchy tunes, and now he wasn't there anymore. Dan and Gaz argued non-stop about the direction to take next. I just did my thing: transporting gear, fixing gear, playing the drums, and keeping my head down. And I was sick of it."

"Dan won, didn't he?" Sherry continued to display her knowledge. "He wrote the second album."

"No." Although they were the only people crammed into the hut, Pete glanced around. "You have to remember I'd left the band by then, but it's an open secret in the industry that Gaz wrote every single one of those songs."

"Odd." Sherry jolted upright, rocking the plastic chair. "Dan alone was credited on the album."

"Yes," Pete said cheerfully. "What a joke. Dan's hopeless at song-writing. But he was the sole member of the band when the album was produced. Jason had gone to a watery grave as far as anyone knew, I'd left, and Gaz had OD'd. Strange that the pressure got to Gaz like that. He wasn't a junkie when we were all together."

"How did the band members deal with drugs?" Neil asked.

"You mean, who did them? Between these four walls, all of us. Dan especially. He'd try anything." A smile played on Pete's lips. "He's done well for himself, squeaky-clean Dan, the singer-songwriter. Granted, he can sing, but the rest is bullshit. Dan popped pills like Smarties, and I doubt he's writing anything. Doing deals with young talent, I'd guess. Gaz could actually knock out a decent tune. It's a shame he died so suddenly, and so young. In a way, I wish I'd stayed and supported him."

"You were telling us why you quit," Neil prompted.

"There's more to life than money. Dan was being obnoxious, he and Gaz quarrelled all the time, and my wife gave me grief for going on the road. I decided rock'n'roll wasn't for me. Then, once the royalty cheques came in for 'Getting High', I started up this business with my brother-in-law."

It took guts to walk away from stardom. Neil wondered if he could bring himself to give up his job for Gemma, or request a transfer to a rural location. He could live without Bristol's eye-watering rent and overpriced nightclubs, but there was a lot he'd miss. It wouldn't be easy to leave Ab's team, coffees with Sherry and craft beer nights with his mates. Sherry was right: he needed to bring Gemma to the city and let its rough-edged charm seduce her.

Meanwhile, Pete was looking smug. "I haven't done too badly, have I?"

That depended how you felt about owning a garage in Bristol's industrial heart rather than a mansion on the edge of London. Pete Willoughby clearly considered he'd made the right choice.

Pete seemed to read his thoughts. "I've no regrets about putting my marriage first. And my kids. We already had Rosie when I packed in the band. I've had three more, and two grandkids, since." Pete rolled up the sleeve of his shabby jumper. "Look, I've got a tattoo for each of them."

Neil wasn't a fan of body art, apart from a cute little daisy chain adorning Gemma's left ankle. He was grateful when Sherry began to gush.

"Cool," Sherry said. "I like that one, especially." She pointed to twin red hearts inked with the names Pete and Lisa.

"I had it done when I got engaged to Lee. We were eighteen and we're still together." Pete beamed. "Anything else you want to know?"

"Did Jason have enemies?" Neil asked. "Did he owe anyone money for drugs, for instance?"

"Not that I'm aware of. He was a likeable guy. Dan still wanted to be friends, even. I mean, Dan had wronged him, but love is blind, I suppose. Not that his affair with Sarah lasted. Dan thought it was her fault that Jason ran off. We all did. I can't understand why he went back to Jackson Crescent, let alone died there. Are you sure the body is his?"

"We're certain," Neil said. A niggling doubt told him that scientists dealt with probabilities, but unless there was a third Jardine brother no-one knew about, they'd got it right.

"I didn't have the time of day for Sarah then," Pete admitted, "but life's too short for grudges. I see her occasionally at a farmers' market. Once, she was having trouble getting her knackered old Land Rover going. I fixed it free of charge. She's not well off."

"She could have used some of Dr Sweet's royalties," Sherry said. "If Ethan is Jason's son, he should have had a share from the first album."

Pete blinked. "That kiddie? I remember him following her around at the market in Clevedon. Nice little lad. Looked like her, I thought. Is he really Jason's boy?"

"Perhaps I misunderstood." Sherry no doubt realised she'd spoken out of turn. After all, Sarah wasn't sure herself.

According to Sarah, Keith Jardine had disowned the lad. He could have been right about Ethan. Maybe he was wrong and had made an honest mistake. A third explanation was more sinister. Keith Jardine had a financial motive: he was receiving royalties as Jason's heir. He might even have killed his son for the money. There was no love lost between them.

Neil's mind raced. It would be both inappropriate and career-limiting to tell Ab what to do. He would have to imitate Sherry, who excelled at subtly planting seeds in the DCI's mind. Somehow, he must suggest to Ab that Keith's story was checked. Had Keith's business really been as successful as he'd claimed, or did he need Jason's royalties to stay afloat?

Pete Willoughby stared at him, his expression inquisitive. Neil realised the mechanic was waiting for him to speak. This was not a man who would jump in to fill a silence. "How often did you go to Jackson Crescent?" he asked Pete.

"A lot, before Jason vanished. Two or three times a week. Afterwards, not at all. Dan wanted to get the band on a more professional footing. He hired a proper rehearsal room in Old Market. It was a relief."

"Why?" Neil asked.

"You took your life in your hands getting in that cellar. Dan loved it because he hardly had to tumble out of bed. He persuaded the rest of us because it was free and soundproof. But you'd almost bend double to get in and out. That was a tunnel built for midgets, or rats, more like. You'd have to dodge stalactites and all sorts. Then there was Mrs Freeman."

"Not Mr Freeman?"

"No, the mad professor was never around. Mrs Freeman worked from home. She would lie in wait to give you a tongue lashing. Snobby bitch. Excuse me, my dear." Pete dipped his chin. "She looked down her nose at me because I wasn't a grammar school boy. She despised Jason even more because he was dark-skinned. Dan told us both to stay out of her way. Quick dash in through the basement door, then down the steps to the cellar."

"You both had keys?"

"One key each. Just for the basement. I gave it back to Dan when he returned from France. He'll tell you," Pete said hopefully.

Dan hadn't mentioned that detail, but he had said Lucy wanted Jason to notice her. "What about Dan's sister?" Neil asked.

"The little girl? I can't even remember her name. Louise, was it? What about her? An antsy teenager, that one."

"What do you mean by antsy, exactly?" Sherry challenged.

"It's what Dan said." Pete shrugged. "She was none too bright, and nosy. Always following us around. She used to watch us rehearse."

"Did she have a crush on one of you, perhaps?" Sherry leaned forward. One of her knees clashed with Neil's.

"Not that she told me. But why would Dan's kid sister confide in me?" Pete pondered for a moment. "Now you mention it, she did hang around Jason a lot."

Pete stared into the distance. Eventually, he said, "Jason was friendly with her, but not over-friendly. He wasn't interested in kiddies. I can't believe he'd have taken advantage."

Through the silent, sickly-sweet air, Neil watched Pete clench and unclench his fists. The mechanic reached for his vape pen again. This time, he didn't request permission.

After a couple of puffs, Pete said, "It's hard to think Jason would stoop so low, not even to get revenge on Dan for stealing Sarah. But he might have done. He might have come back for that. And got himself killed."

"You think Lucy killed him?" Neil asked, eager to hear his suspicions confirmed.

"Lucy. Of course, that was her name." Pete shook his head. "No. She was just a kid."

Really? Neil thought. As a thirteen-year-old, Lucy was doing drugs and chasing a man ten years older. All the signs pointed to a teenager out of control. He wished Ab would listen to his concerns. How could he persuade his boss they should dig deeper into her story?

Pete hadn't finished. "Lucy would have been thrilled to see him. Her lover, back from the dead, coming all the way from France for her. It's sickening, but imagine you're an adolescent girl.

You'd find it romantic. Trust me on this. I've raised kids and I know how their minds work."

"We don't always think straight at that age," Sherry admitted.

"You see?" Pete's beady eyes glittered. "And before you ask, I don't think Dan murdered Jason, either. Wasn't he stuck in France for weeks, with the gendarmes? He wouldn't have cared, anyhow. If it kept Jason sweet, it'd be all right with Dan. No. I bet Mrs Freeman caught Jason and Lucy together. That bitch would have gone ballistic."

CHAPTER 20

LUCY

The journalists had returned. Buzzing like bees around a hive, they had gathered outside number 13, quizzing anyone who happened to pass. Lucy had turned away at least half a dozen from the door. Always, she used the same mantra: "No comment. We don't know anything."

After the first couple of times, she had gone online and discovered the police had made a statement. The skeleton's identity was confirmed as Jason Jardine, the missing bassist from Dr Sweet. He had been found in a cellar accessible from number 13 Jackson Crescent, the home of Sebastian and Jennifer Freeman. The public were asked to get in touch if they had ever visited the cellar, or knew why and when Jason had done so.

Lucy bristled with indignation. The police should have told the family their address had been given to the media. She texted Sebastian, who was at the university, and presumably oblivious to this development. Then she realised Jennifer would be interested, and switched on the TV for the local news.

Lucy couldn't bear to stay in the sitting room and watch it herself. Like a knife twisting in her guts, it reminded her, over and over again, that Jason was dead. She busied herself tidying Jennifer's bedroom, then offered to make tea.

Jennifer didn't reply, of course. If she could, she would doubtless have accepted. The old Jennifer drank strong black coffee at business meetings to appear one of the boys, but tea was what she preferred. To her, it was a convivial drink over which the world could be put to rights.

To Lucy, it represented comfort. Trembling as she retreated to the kitchen, she needed the steadying influence of a cuppa. After splashing water on her face to calm down, she put the kettle on. She placed teabags in a pot and added boiling water: mundane tasks she wouldn't normally even think about. Today, she had to concentrate and take them one step at a time. She laid the pot on a tray with milk jug, spoons, and sipping cup. On impulse, she added a Wedgwood cup and saucer for herself. Then, carefully, she carried the tray upstairs.

The TV bulletin had moved on to football. That wouldn't entertain Jennifer, who was indifferent to the division of Bristol's loyalties north and south of the river. Lucy switched it off.

"Here, Mum. I've made tea the proper way," she said. It wasn't strictly true; at school, she had been taught to warm the pot first and to use leaves. She hoped Jennifer enjoyed seeing the china put into service, though. Tenderly, she filled the sipping cup with tea, cooling it down with milk. She tested it on the back of her hand. "Still too hot. Give it ten minutes. Would you like to see some old photos?"

Sebastian often sat with Jennifer to flick through their picture albums, especially photographs of their early married life in Singapore. He had been advised by their GP that it would help Jennifer keep her memories alive, as would wearing her old clothes and perfume.

Jennifer's limbs jerked. She groaned.

"That's a yes, isn't it? I'll pour my tea, then we'll start." Lucy finished serving herself. She reached for a book of party snapshots. Jennifer had been enviably slim, elegant and effervescent in her cocktail dresses.

Sasha, snoozing in a corner, pricked up her ears and barked. The doorbell was ringing again, first a short burst, then a longer one.

"Sorry, Mum. It'll be another reporter." Dog at her heels, Lucy prepared to rebuff them.

The man standing outside wasn't what she expected. Rather than springing forward with questions, he stood back from the threshold and smiled. Beneath an expensive-looking dark wool coat, he wore a suit, shirt and tie. His black shoes were polished. He was immaculately groomed, nails tidily cut and grey hair short over a bald pate. Lucy caught a whiff of spicy cologne.

She found herself drawn to him, the words of rejection dying in her mouth. There was something familiar about him that she couldn't place. Maybe it was the cologne, or the way his hair curled at the side of his forehead. Daniel's did too. Jennifer had called it a cowlick. It was the only aspect of her son that Jennifer had belittled.

"I'd like to see Jennifer Freeman, please. I'm an old friend, Brett Hollande. She may have mentioned me." His voice sounded rich and cultured. He turned his palms towards her, as if to prove his sincerity.

Lucy fidgeted. She didn't have the heart to say that Jennifer had never spoken about him at all.

Brett glanced at his watch, which Lucy now saw was a Rolex. That clinched it for her. Reporters didn't have that kind of money.

Sasha jumped up at him, tongue ready to lick.

"Mrs Freeman is in, isn't she?" Brett asked, gently pushing the dog back. He obviously thought Lucy was the hired help.

"I'm her daughter, Lucy." Seeing newsmen beginning to cluster behind him, Lucy added, "You'd better come in."

The dog, grasping that Brett wouldn't make a fuss of her, padded into the sitting room.

Lucy closed the door behind Brett, standing in his way to stop him following Sasha. "You haven't seen Mum for a while, I guess. Did you know about her illness?"

Brett said with alarm, "No, I didn't. What's happened?"

He emoted sympathy and concern. Lucy was almost tempted to hug him. It occurred to her that she hadn't actually told him Jennifer was alive.

"Mum has Parkinson's. It's late stages." She stumbled over the words. "So she's fine, but she's not as – functional – as you might remember."

"How very sad." Brett's gaze fixed Lucy's, his brown eyes wide. "I should explain. It has been decades since I saw your mother. We were very dear friends, then we lost touch. I was in the area – I am staying in Stokes Croft. Do you know it? Very hip, I believe – and I saw the news reports. It must be most upsetting to have a body turn up in your backyard. That made me think I really should visit to offer my support."

How kind he was. She felt guilty for assuming he was a reporter.

"By the way, how's your father?" Brett asked. "I remember meeting him at university gatherings early in his academic career. A lovely man."

"He's in good health. I'm sorry, he's at the university at the moment."

Relief flashed through Brett's eyes so fast that it was gone before Lucy could blink.

"What a shame I've missed him," Brett said.

"I'll take you to Mum." Lucy led him to Jennifer's sitting room, catching the dog in the act of sniffing at the tea tray.

"Not for you," Lucy said to the animal, ignoring the huff she received in reply.

"Jennifer." Brett's face lit up as he approached her wing chair. "How lovely to see you. You look well."

It was true, Lucy thought, if you ignored Jennifer's distant stare. Each morning, her mother was dressed in flattering clothes, her make-up carefully applied. It was the least Lucy could do for her. 'If you look good, you feel good,' Jennifer had always said. Lucy hoped her mother still believed it.

Brett evidently hadn't expected a total lack of response. "Jennifer?" he said.

Lucy squirmed. "I'm sorry. I did try to tell you. Intellectually, Mum is 100%, but her movement and speech aren't great."

Jennifer's mouth twitched. No sound emerged, although she clearly recognised Brett. It was reassuring.

"Would you like tea, Brett?" Lucy asked. "You can have this one; I haven't touched it. I'll fetch another."

She handed him her cup and saucer. Her mother would have to go without until Brett left. Jennifer's plastic beaker would still be too hot. Anyway, Lucy was uneasy about giving it to her mother in front of him. It was a question of Jennifer's dignity, however close she might have been to Brett in the past. Lucy shuddered. Sometimes her imagination got the better of her.

Brett thanked her for the tea. It was perfect, just as he liked it, and he was sorry to put her to the trouble. He sat on the sofa opposite Jennifer and began to deliver a monologue of small talk.

Lucy made to leave the room. As if an unseen hand had turned a key, Sasha sprang to her feet. She skittered ahead of Lucy, into the hall and down the stairs. Evidently, the dog sensed the kitchen was Lucy's destination. There, the animal sat mournfully by her empty food and water bowls.

"I suppose it's nearly lunchtime," Lucy conceded. She filled both containers, slipping in a slice of ham with the unappetising dried pellets Margaret had provided for the dog.

The Samoyed reacted enthusiastically. A stranger would imagine she hadn't been fed for a week.

Laughing, Lucy returned to the sitting room. "I forgot to offer you sugar," she said to Brett, "but I've brought it now. Would you like some?"

"No, thank you." Brett's lips were set in a tight line. He set down his teacup and rose to his feet.

A wave of understanding hit Lucy. He must feel so lost, coming to see an old friend and finding Jennifer in this limbo. She stood up too, sympathy impelling her to place a hand on his arm. "You see?" she began to say.

She didn't finish. Brett evaded her, marching not to the door, but the sash window overlooking the garden. His fisted hands, knuckles white, rested on the console table in front of it.

Lucy wondered if he was about to faint. "Would you like another cup of tea?" she asked, barely succeeding in keeping her voice level. She was imagining the crack as his head hit the marble table, blood on the carpet and the impossibility of explaining it all to the granite-faced detective. "There's no cake but you could have a piece of chocolate." Her mother wouldn't approve of that, but Jennifer was in no position to vocalise her complaints.

Brett turned slowly, one hand still drawing support from the table. His eyes fixed hers. "That won't be necessary. I'm okay. It's just a shock."

"My brother always says that."

"Brother?"

"You know – Daniel." If he didn't know, how could he be her mother's friend? Lucy looked down, breaking eye contact. An inner voice berated her. She wasn't a teenager; she shouldn't be overwhelmed by awkwardness.

Brett nodded. "How is Daniel?"

"Okay." She shrugged. "I don't hear much from him. He's too busy being a rock star."

A strange expression, conceivably one of hope, flitted across Brett's face. "Of course. Dr Sweet," he said. "Well, give my regards to your father." Finally, he made for the hallway.

Lucy had forgotten the dog. Sasha had apparently decided that Brett had ignored her for too long. With a loud bark, she raced up the stairs, flinging herself at the man's legs before Lucy could stop her.

Brett tripped over.

"Bad dog. Brett, I'm so, so sorry." Lucy held out an arm to him.

Occupied by the dog, Brett didn't take it. He flailed, trying and failing to stand.

Her breath faltered for a split-second. Brett's shoes were highly polished and expensive-looking, but the soles were worn to a sliver. Lucy glimpsed a hole temporarily fixed with newspaper. That wouldn't keep Brett's feet dry when it rained. It didn't make sense for a man of his means. Perhaps these were an old pair he loved and couldn't bear to discard.

Brett allowed the dog to lick his face before turfing the animal off his lap. "I really must go. It's been lovely to meet you. You're not at all what I'd expect Jennifer's daughter to be like."

No, she didn't suppose she was, Lucy thought bitterly. He would have imagined a clone of Jennifer in the old days: thin, pretty, and witty.

Brett looked at his watch again, studying it for so long that Lucy wondered if the dog had broken it. Thankfully, Brett said nothing. With a quick farewell, he dived out of the front door and into the fray. As far as she could tell, he didn't stop to talk to the media.

It was a pity he had made his way to Jackson Crescent only to find Jennifer so uncommunicative. Lucy said as much to her mother, making sure she didn't appear to be casting blame. It was hardly Jennifer's fault.

"Would you like your tea now?" Lucy picked up the sipping cup. It was tepid, but not unpleasant.

"C-count."

Lucy nearly dropped the beaker. "What did you say?"

Jennifer stared vacantly at the window. A fleck of spittle bubbled from her lips. How could she have spoken? Yet it was the voice Lucy remembered, rather than the garbled whispers she'd become used to.

Jennifer coughed and began to wheeze. Lucy gaped at her. There had been no sign of illness earlier, apart from her mother's chronic condition. Jennifer hadn't taken so much as a drop of tea, either. She couldn't have swallowed a foreign object. Why, then, was she struggling to breathe?

Time stretched. Lucy became aware of her own breath sounding in short gasps. She tried to slow it down, desperately scouring her brain for remnants of her limited first aid training. A sudden burst of adrenaline lent her clarity. She patted Jennifer's back. It made no difference. Lucy increased the pressure until she was thumping Jennifer's spine.

"I'm so sorry." She must be hurting her mother, yet to no avail.

Sasha whined and nuzzled Jennifer's slippered feet, giving up when nobody took any notice. Out of the corner of her eye, Lucy spotted the dog at the coffee table, licking the dregs of the teacups. One of them crashed to the floor.

Lucy winced at the sound. "Sorry," she repeated, tension seething through her and stiffening her limbs. She fumbled for the pulse at

Jennifer's wrist. Surely the heartbeat was faster than normal? Her mother's hand felt cold and clammy. Could it be a heart attack? Whatever it was, she'd reached the limit of her ability to deal with it. If only Brett had stayed five minutes longer.

Jennifer's chest heaved, air emerging from it in rattles and rasps. Despite the make-up, her skin took on a waxy cast. She continued to stare, her basilisk gaze seeming to find Lucy wanting.

Lucy felt a tear splash down her cheek. "I'll get help," she told her mother, voice trembling. Her hands shook as she reached into a pocket for her phone. Sobbing, she tapped in 999.

"I need an ambulance… for my mother… it's her heart."

"Cheer up," Sebastian told Lucy. "It could have been worse."

She sniffed, trying not to cry. If her father could put on a brave face, so could she. He still looked as exhausted as she felt, nerves shattered after spending all day at the Bristol Royal Infirmary. Following her cardiac arrest, Jennifer was being kept in for observation. There was talk of fitting a stent. Jennifer was alive, but hardly well.

Night had fallen long ago. When visiting hours ended, Sebastian had bought sandwiches in the hospital's small Marks & Spencer's shop, then they had taken a taxi home together.

Back in a dark and silent Jackson Crescent, Sebastian unlocked the front door. The dog, lying in the unlit hallway, bounced up to them as if on springs. After barking furiously, Sasha ran outside, watered the front yard, and returned.

"The poor thing has been alone for hours." Guilt needled at Lucy. She'd paid no heed to the dog earlier. There had barely been time to pack Jennifer's bag and follow her stretchered form into the ambulance.

"We can make it up to Sasha." Sebastian opened a packet of sandwiches and gave a triangle to the pet. "Here, let's share. And don't tell Margaret."

Lucy eyed the other half, suddenly ravenous. Trailing around the hospital after Jennifer, she hadn't thought about food.

Sebastian evidently felt the same. He switched on the light in Jennifer's sitting room. "Let's eat in here. The dog can clear up the crumbs. Oh dear, what happened?"

"The dog tried to clear up the tea." A broken cup lay on the floor, reproaching Lucy. Luckily, it had only fractured at the handle joint; she should be able to mend it. Before bedtime, she must tidy everything away.

Her gaze flicked to the console table and its three golden monkeys. Only two statues gleamed back at her, hands clapped to their eyes or ears.

"Is that what you meant, Mum? Count the monkeys?"

Sebastian grimaced. "Pardon? Or were you talking to yourself, Lucy?"

"Harry's missing, Dad."

Her father looked sceptical. "Surely not. He probably just fell off."

Lucy crouched down, checking under the table. She scanned the sideboard nearby. "I can't see him." Her cheeks burned, as she realised it was all her fault. She hadn't noticed the figure being spirited away. "Brett was standing right here earlier. I bet he stole Harry."

Sebastian raised an eyebrow. "Stole? That's a strong word. Who is Brett, anyway?"

"Brett Hollande. You know, Mum's old friend."

"Who?"

"He visited earlier. He——." She attempted to collect her thoughts about Brett: the odd sense of recognition, the suspicion that he didn't know

Jennifer as well as he claimed, and now the statue's disappearance. Once or twice, she'd spotted a resemblance to Daniel. Brett's hairline was similar. He, too, had a way of coming across as your best friend when he smiled. Perhaps he was a distant relative. Lucy had never met her mother's side of the family. Years before her birth, they had cut off contact with Jennifer, apparently jealous that she had married so well.

"He had the look of family," she said. "I guessed he might be Mum's cousin. A half-brother, even."

Sebastian shook his head. "She only has sisters. Jen never mentioned a cousin called Brett, either."

"He said he'd met you."

"A former colleague of hers? I was her plus one at work events." Sebastian shuddered. "How odd that he decided to look her up just now, when Jason Jardine's body has been found under the garden. It makes you think he might know how it got there."

She hadn't considered that. Why, if he were the murderer, would Brett revisit the scene of the crime? The obvious answer was that Jennifer knew about it and he wished to ensure her silence.

Why, then, was he irritated that she couldn't speak?

"Brett claimed he'd heard about Jason. He wanted to offer Mum his support," she said.

"That's good of him," Sebastian replied drily. "And you trusted him?"

"He seemed nice. But he had tatty shoes, and Harry's gone."

Her father sighed. When he eventually spoke, his tone was not unkind. "I suspect we're both overtired and overthinking things. Tatty shoes don't make anyone a killer or thief. The cleaner probably moved Harry somewhere."

Lucy chewed her lip. "I'll just tidy up, then I'm going to bed."

It was always the same. He didn't believe her, and nor did anyone else. She withdrew to the kitchen, making fresh tea for herself and gobbling her sandwich. Afterwards, she retrieved a large bar of milk chocolate hidden behind vases in a corner cupboard. Savagely, she tore off the paper cover, unwrapping two squares from the foil within. She bit down on the chocolate, indulging in the rich, creamy taste. Happiness and confidence surged through her. Hungry for the golden moment to last, Lucy devoured the rest of the bar and hid the evidence in the bin. She shivered with pleasure.

It took mere minutes for the sweetness to vanish from her tongue. Self-hatred hit her with the intensity of a slap in the face. She had eaten a full hundred grammes. That was like a McDonald's quarter-pounder made entirely from chocolate. The thought of fast food sickened her, but she couldn't help imagining a McDonald's quarter-pounder chocolate dessert. For that, she would brave the smell of chips and vinegar, the jeers and stares of skinnier customers. Fat slobs like her, morons like her, stupid people who nobody believed, would reach for comfort food like that. Hot tears stung her face, splashing into her tea.

CHAPTER 21

LUCY

It was nearly midnight and Lucy had finished crying. Daniel didn't pick up the phone or reply to her frantic texts. Situation normal, she thought. Sighing, she tidied the kitchen. Her footsteps seemed to echo as she mounted the stairs to her bedroom. Although Jennifer would usually be asleep by now, the house felt vast and empty without her.

She Googled Daniel and swiftly found proof he was in the UK. He'd been papped at a billionaire's ball in London earlier in the evening. Daniel, smiling boyishly next to his latest starlet girlfriend, had claimed he wouldn't have missed this party for the world. He made time for his friends, if not his family.

The day had been like a rollercoaster, picking up speed and crashing harder and faster each time. It had begun with the media's low level harassment, then Brett's arrival, and finally the agonising fear that Jennifer would die and it would be Lucy's fault. Yet Jennifer, luckily, was alive.

Daniel had to be persuaded to visit his mother. His presence would comfort her and possibly hasten her recovery. Also, what if the worst happened? Daniel would want to be there, wouldn't he?

Nausea gripped her suddenly, a sour taste of bile rising in her throat. Perhaps Daniel didn't wish to return. He could be ignoring her texts on purpose, determined to enjoy his shiny life and forget an inconveniently dying mother. After all, he'd barely bothered with Jennifer during her years of illness.

She realised Daniel and Brett resembled each other in more than looks. They were both polite and charming. They both used people. Brett had left the house as soon as he'd pocketed an item of value. He must have always intended to steal something, or at least ask for money. Daniel had taken what he needed from his parents: the expensive education and the subsidies as he fought his way into the music business. Then he'd moved on. You could love your brother, she decided, without being blind to his faults.

In the distance, the Clifton College clock chimed twelve times. A blinding headache added to Lucy's woes. Gaming was out of the question.

Anyway, Xander was trying to get too close to her. He would ask her how she was. She didn't care to have that conversation with anyone right now, and maybe never with Xander at all. She didn't need or want friends. Like Daniel, they would flit away to a better life, leaving a void larger than the sinkhole. As she snuggled under her duvet, head throbbing, she hoped Jennifer wouldn't abandon her too.

Overwhelmed with fatigue, she still couldn't sleep. Reluctantly, she shrugged off the duvet, goosebumps rising as the chilly air hit her skin. She crept down the creaking staircase. Sasha, dozing by the front door, sprang to her feet.

"Sorry, Sasha," Lucy whispered, stroking the velvety fur between the animal's ears. She located strong painkillers in Jennifer's bedroom and tiptoed back upstairs. Finally, the tablets quietened her buzzing brain. She slipped into a deep slumber.

The next morning, brain foggy, she showered and dressed before she remembered Jennifer was in hospital. The headache returned. Lucy took more painkillers.

Her father was already up and sitting at the kitchen table with a cafetière, a break from the usual routine of taking black coffee into his study. The dog napped at his feet, evidently having breakfasted.

"I've phoned the hospital," Sebastian said. "She's doing well and we can visit again this afternoon. Any word from Daniel? I haven't been able to reach him."

Lucy shook her head. "I couldn't either last night, Dad. I'll try later. Would you like toast?"

"No, thanks. I've got work to do." He yawned, stood up and disappeared into his study.

This was how Sebastian dealt with stress, by closeting himself away to consider the great ethical issues of the day. In contrast, Lucy reached for food. As soon as she heard his study door slam, she placed two slices of bread in the toaster. When they were done, she buttered them and made a sandwich with squares of clandestine chocolate. Her mouth salivated at the first bite. Nothing else mattered while she ate the crispy, gooey treat. Then it was over and guilt nudged her like an old friend.

She'd have to use the calories taking Sasha for a longer walk. It would help her to forget her

249

mother's absence. As well as the huge gap in Lucy's routine, there was an aching fear that it would become permanent. How would her life have a purpose without Jennifer to love and care for? Sobbing, she clasped Sasha around the middle. The dog snuggled into her. She drank in the sweet scent of Sasha's fur, finally calming down enough to ring Daniel again.

This time, he picked up. "I'm busy, sis. Can't talk."

She almost dropped the phone. Clutching it, she said, "You can't talk? But you must have seen my texts. Mum's really ill."

"She'll get over it." Daniel's voice was strained. "Listen, I'm super-busy. Got to make a ton of phone calls this morning and sort out paperwork for my tour."

"Don't you have people to do that?" It stretched credibility that a millionaire like Daniel would carry out such basic tasks himself.

"I'm working on it. There's a PA with me." His tone sweetened. "Yes, Alicia, put it there. As I was about to say, Lucy, I sacked my manager yesterday. He ripped me off once too often."

Why would the office staff go with him? She had such a limited knowledge of workplaces, she wasn't sure what was normal. The dispute with his manager didn't come across as strange. This must have been his tenth, or was it the twelfth? At least one had died of an overdose, prompting more headlines of the 'Doomed Dr Sweet' variety. Daniel had never discussed it with her, of course. All she knew was what she'd read as she surfed through online clickbait.

A plan began to form. "Where are you?" she asked.

"At home. Where else?" Clearly exasperated, Daniel huffed. "Look, I've got to go."

He cut the call. She was left staring at the silent phone.

Once Lucy was resolved, it hadn't taken long to persuade her father that he should take the dog for its morning walk. He wasn't averse to visiting Jennifer alone, either. Sebastian gave the impression of a man bereft. He had cancelled his lectures to spend time with his wife. Lucy suspected he would read her more Aristotle. Her father remained convinced that, having studied for a philosophy degree, her mother was fascinated by the subject. Despite this, Lucy had never seen Jennifer pick up one of his textbooks. Her third-class degree hardly signalled much interest either. Daniel had once told Lucy that Jennifer only passed because Sebastian had fiddled her results. Their mother, he'd said, had viewed the philosophy course as a route to a rich husband.

How had Daniel known that, and why had he divulged it to her? Maybe it was for the same reason he'd shown her the garden cellar, because he found it exciting to share a secret. Whatever his motive then, she was determined to talk to him about Jennifer again. There would be no gossip this time. She would guilt-trip him into visiting the hospital.

She could have an adventure too. A train journey meant nothing to Sebastian and Daniel, world-weary travellers for whom even a transatlantic flight was mundane. To Lucy, buying a ticket and navigating the crowds at Bristol Temple Meads station took her well outside her comfort zone.

It had been more daunting, years ago, when she had set off for university in one of London's less prepossessing dormitory towns. She had barely scraped into the former technical college to do a creative arts foundation course. Scarily, she'd had to pass through London alone on her first journey there. Other students had been driven by their parents, she later discovered, but Sebastian had been away at a conference and Jennifer was too busy.

London had no central station serving all railway lines. Lucy had to take the Tube across town, teetering on deep escalators. Initially, she caught a train going in the wrong direction. It was the rush hour. Pressed tightly into the carriage by strangers, she'd gone past three stops before she had the courage to fight her way to the door. Meanwhile, more passengers crammed themselves inside. She'd imagined the metal walls bursting.

It was almost a relief when she'd flunked her first year exams, to no-one's surprise. You needed more than a passable voice to make it as a musician, Jennifer had told her. Talent, looks and presence were required. Daniel was proof of that.

Since then, she'd been on the Tube half a dozen times, but the thought of it still made her shudder. Fortunately, she could avoid the capital today. Changing trains at Reading, she took a service to Richmond, then a cab to Daniel's mansion. The driver mistook her for a groupie and drily wished her luck. She didn't bother to correct him. There was such a contrast between Daniel's sleek dark looks and her plump milkmaid appearance that he wouldn't have believed they were siblings. She was proud to have made it this far. The biggest challenge lay ahead: persuading Daniel to return to Bristol.

The taxi driver honked his horn and drove away as she peered through the railings. Daniel's black and white house was picture-perfect with its mullioned windows and frosty garden. The sight reminded Lucy of an old woodcut, or perhaps an illustration from a fairy-tale. On the drive, a low-slung red car introduced a modern note.

Lucy had been there only once before. When Daniel bought the property, Sebastian had driven the family from Bristol to see it. Jennifer, her old, brisk self, had inspected every detail and complimented her son on his taste. Daniel had said airily that he didn't expect to be there often. He'd repeated the comment whenever Lucy suggested they should meet in Richmond.

She had paid no attention to the high railings and gate on that first visit. Daniel had probably been waiting for them then. Lucy couldn't remember Sebastian ringing a doorbell. She was looking around for one when a scream cut through the still air.

The sharp, short sound had come from the house. She was sure of it. Even as quiet descended once more, Lucy knew she hadn't imagined that chilling cry. Her eyes flicked to the taxi retreating around the corner, then to a buzzer by the locked gate. Taking a deep breath, she pasted an appeasing smile on her face and pressed the button.

The front door opened. A giant of a man raced through it. With a click and a clang, the gate began to swivel inwards.

Lucy recognised Jeff, the minder. She marched into the garden, maintaining her smile and trying to look confident as he ran towards her. "Hi. I'm Daniel's sister. Remember?"

"I don't care if you're the Queen, love." He dashed past and into the street.

Lucy gawped in dismay. "I thought I heard a scream. What happened?"

"Nothing to do with me," he spat. "It's above my pay grade."

"What about my brother?" she yelled at his retreating back. "You're supposed to be protecting him."

The gate began to close again. Lucy hesitated, watching the gap narrow. Within that house lurked somebody or something so dangerous that hard-bitten Jeff couldn't deal with it. It wasn't sensible to ignore so clear a warning. Yet the cry of distress had sounded like Daniel. His bodyguard had deserted her brother, but she couldn't.

As the gate clanked shut, she glanced regretfully at the street. There was no escape route. The high security, designed to keep trouble out of Daniel's property, had trapped her within. Tension stiffening her shoulders, she crept up to the house, flinching when her feet crunched on the gravel path.

The front door was still ajar. Tentatively, Lucy pushed it. She almost stopped when she heard a man whisper, "No," but she was committed now. Daniel needed her, didn't he?

Her senses exploded as soon as she walked inside. "Daniel?" she gasped at her brother.

He stood squarely in the hallway, facing her, anger blazing in his eyes. Between him and the door, another man staggered backwards, nearly colliding with her. He swayed around.

"Brett! Goodness, what happened?" She took a step back. As before, Jennifer's old friend was impeccably turned out, which only emphasised the blood spreading across his white shirt.

Brett's gaze fixed hers, imploring. His voice, hoarse and horrifyingly liquid, rasped, "Help... me. See... what he's done."

Daniel's lip curled. "Did you see what Jeff did, Lucy?" he demanded. "Thank God you're here. I've got to get Brett to hospital."

"I'll ring 999." She reached into her bag.

"Help... it was..." Brett's eyes glazed over, his face ashen. He slumped against her. She gagged at the smell of blood filling her nostrils: a butcher's shop tang, metallic and raw.

"Daniel, please stop him falling. I have to call an ambulance."

"There's no time, sis. My Ferrari is much faster. I'll take him." Daniel yanked the older man to his feet. "Help me get his arm over my shoulder."

"The wound is still bleeding," she said. "He needs first aid. Sit him down. Have you got bandages?"

"No, he needs a doctor, for God's sake. We're wasting time. Are you going to help me or not?"

Lucy gave in. She'd never persuade her brother to listen to her, and she didn't doubt he'd drive quickly. Brett would be with medical professionals within minutes. She grabbed the injured man's arm and draped it around the back of Daniel's neck.

Daniel began to drag Brett to the door. "There. Brett, I can get you to the car now. Come on."

Brett was barely conscious. Blood bubbled from his lips.

Instinctively, Lucy wiped her hands on her jacket. She fished tissues from her handbag, using the stain on Brett's shirt to guide her as she pressed them to his chest. "We must staunch the flow."

Trying to hold the flimsy paper in place, she scurried alongside Daniel as he hauled Brett outside. To her despair, gore soaked through the wad of tissues within seconds.

"Forget it, sis," Daniel growled. "That didn't work and you're slowing me down."

With her free hand, she unwound her woolly scarf and used that instead. "Hopefully, that will stop it a bit."

"I'm sure it will." Daniel's sharp tone suggested impatience. "Look, can you open the passenger door? It isn't locked."

"How?"

"Contactless. The key's in my pocket."

As she feared, the sodden scarf fell to the ground as soon as she let go of it. She followed her brother's instructions, though. There was no way he could carry Brett and open the car by himself. How would he have coped if she hadn't turned up?

The vehicle was a two-seater, of course. She couldn't accompany them and would just have to trust her brother's common sense. Holding the door for him, she watched Daniel manhandle Brett inside it. The older man's head lolled alarmingly.

"Daniel, you shouldn't move him like that!"

He scowled. "For God's sake. Can I just get him in the car?"

"Why did Jeff—?" she finally asked.

"Self-defence. I'll bring you up to speed later." Daniel opened the driver's door and sat behind the wheel. "Go inside and clean yourself up."

He slammed the door and started the engine. The gate opened. Like a flash of red lightning, the car roared off the drive and out of sight.

Lucy shivered. At first, she thought the biting wind had affected her. Then, when she couldn't stop, she realised it was the awful strangeness of the situation. Brett's shocking injury and Daniel's coldness were totally at odds. She suspected Jeff had punctured his victim's lung. A first aid kit and instructions from the emergency services might have improved Brett's chances, at least while they waited for an ambulance. Daniel had hardly taken heed when she suggested it, though. He'd had Brett's interests at heart, but she wished she'd insisted on calling 999.

With horror, she saw the crimson stains over her hands, anorak, and jeans. Daniel was right: she needed to wash the blood off everything. Anyone seeing her would call the police, and how would she explain her condition to them? Suppose word got back to the suspicious DC Neil Slater in Bristol? Anxiously, Lucy scanned the road. No vehicles drove past, no lace curtains twitched. No-one sprang out of Daniel's home, or any other. It was as peaceful as it had been before Brett screamed.

She returned inside, noting just a few drops of blood on the floor as evidence of Brett's trauma. Skirting round them, Lucy found a cloakroom off the hall. She remembered this as large and glitzy. Even in normal circumstances she would feel out of place amid the spotlights and mirrors. She stumbled, bumping her shins on an easy chair when she caught a glimpse of herself. Straggly hair, stained clothing and a darkening smear on her cheek contrasted with her plush surroundings.

Lucy removed her jacket and lathered soap on her face and hands. An aroma of lilies countered the bloody reek. After washing, she dried herself with a luxurious white towel. Moistening the fluffy cotton, she added a dollop of liquid soap and began to scrub her jeans. Somehow, she'd have to dry them before going back outside. Here, the atmosphere was tropical, heat rising from the marble floor. Wearing wet clothes almost seemed pleasant. Out in the street, she'd be risking hypothermia.

She turned her attention to her parka, a peach colour on which the reddish-brown marks were all too visible. Its label advised dry cleaning only. Lucy daubed soapy water on it anyway. She succeeded only in smudging the gore. At that point, she gave up.

Flinging herself onto the chair, she sat with her head in her hands. How and why had Brett tracked down Daniel? Yesterday, the older man had hardly been aware of her brother's existence. Lucy supposed that, scenting money, Brett had researched Dr Sweet and approached Daniel with a begging bowl.

Jeff had seemed terrified. It didn't square with his tough guy image. Despite acting in self-defence, he might have been afraid of the police. She wasn't about to call them but she'd have to ask Daniel if he intended to. Meanwhile, she texted her brother. When would he come home, she asked, and how was Brett now?

It felt like hours of angst before she heard the beep of a reply, but it was really no more than ten minutes. "All fine. Back in 20. Make urself comfy. Have a drink."

She steeled herself to use the towel to clean the red streaks she'd left all over the cloakroom. When she'd finished, she used it to mop the hall floor, just in case anyone slipped. Lucy doubted Daniel's staff were around, though, as surely they would have heard the commotion with Brett?

She ventured into the largest reception room, thankful to see logs burning in the grate. Edgily, she sat on the sofa nearest the fire, attempting to process her thoughts. Steam rose from her jeans as they dried.

She might not hold the moral high ground over Daniel anymore. Daniel would be worried about Brett, so should she really push her brother to visit Jennifer? Yet whoever Brett really was, relative or not, he'd arrived with nefarious motives. Daniel's responsibilities towards him ended at the hospital door.

Her legs no longer damp, Lucy hunted down a cup of tea. The Harrods teabags in Daniel's huge kitchen made an acceptable brew, ideal for dunking the more downmarket Rich Tea biscuits she also found.

The silence within the house came as a relief. She didn't fancy explaining either her presence or the bloodied coat to Daniel's heavies. Where were they, or the servants who cooked for her brother and kept the place tidy? She curled up on the sofa, ears twitching for sounds of life.

Daniel's return was heralded by the purr of his sports car outside. Shortly afterwards, he appeared, looking remarkably unruffled. There wasn't a spot of blood on his cream cashmere jumper.

"I need a drink," he announced, pouring himself a single malt. He downed it in one and refilled his glass. "Want some?"

"I've got tea." She blurted out, "Where are your people? And especially, why did Jeff run away?"

He raised an eyebrow. "I told you. I sacked my manager. Staffing was her responsibility. And Jeff panicked because he realised he'd gone too far when Brett threw a punch at me. I'd have fired him anyhow, for accepting a mad story from that fruitcake and letting him in. But tell me. You knew Brett's name. Who is he?"

His manager had been a woman. That was news. Lucy wondered if there had been a romantic angle.

"Well, Lucy? You were telling me about Brett," he prompted.

"I don't know him. But he came round to see Mum yesterday. He—" About to say Brett had stolen Harry, she was silenced by the hatred glittering in Daniel's eyes.

"Mum had a heart attack, right? He must have caused it. The scumbag."

Lucy gasped. She hadn't considered that. Her dislike of Brett deepened in spite of her pity for him. "How is he? Where did you take him?" she asked.

"He's at the hospital. Honestly, he's fine. Just a scratch." Daniel glowered.

It had shown signs of being worse. Medics knew better than her, though.

"He knows exactly what I think of him." Daniel paced beside the cocktail cabinet, his jaw tense. "I told him if he bothers Mum anymore, I'm calling the police. He got the message. We won't hear from him again, sis."

"He took Harry. One of the wise monkeys."

Daniel's eyes narrowed. "If you'd said, I bet I could have got it back. No chance of that now."

Lucy cringed. That familiar feeling of being wrong swept over her. She recalled the hope that had flitted across Brett's face when he heard Jennifer's son was a rock star. "I'm sorry, I should have realised he'd visit you. Brett looks a bit like you, and I thought he might be a relation. As in Mum's long-lost secret brother or something."

For a second, Daniel appeared startled. Then he laughed. "Now you're being melodramatic. No, he's just a crazy, that's all. Good riddance."

"Why did he attack you?"

"I asked him to leave. Actually, I told Jeff to throw him out." Daniel winced. "I didn't expect Jeff to assault him with a paper knife. Luckily for him, Brett won't be pressing charges. We'll clean up in here and no-one will know it ever happened."

That reminded her. "I've left my coat in your cloakroom. The blood wouldn't wash out."

Daniel set down his glass, sat beside Lucy and hugged her. "I'd forgotten how awful this was for you. Drink some whisky. And I'll get new clothes couriered here within the hour. They won't cost you a penny, and before you start protesting, I insist. Now what's your size?"

"Erm." She swallowed. "I'm afraid it's 16."

His blank stare indicated that it meant nothing to him. His girlfriends probably all wore size zero, or minus numbers if they existed. Lucy was firmly on the plus side.

"I'll make a phone call," he said, fetching a glass. "This whisky is Laphroaig, but I have others if you prefer?"

"It's fine." Although she'd sworn never to drink whisky again after her first teenage hangover, perhaps it would help her calm down. Anyway, it saved an argument.

The drink he poured for her was smokier than the blends her father liked, but still too familiar. As memories of her last meeting with Jason flooded back, she felt sick. The whisky had been a mistake. Lucy almost spat out the first fiery sip. She had to make herself swallow it. When Daniel left the room to make a phone call, she threw the rest on the fire. Its flames briefly burned blue, then blazed bright yellow once more.

Her brother returned and spotted the empty glass. "There. That's better, isn't it? I've just called a local boutique. They'll bring you a few things in twenty minutes."

"Thank you." She still felt unsteady, but she had to broach the subject of a visit before the salespeople arrived. "Daniel, I'm so worried about Mum. If you came to the hospital, even for half an hour, it would really perk her up."

"Sis, you're such a sweet talker. I'll visit if I can, but no guarantees. I need to get over this terrible mess with Brett first. Maybe I can clear my diary in a couple of days, okay?"

She nodded. Half a promise was better than a refusal.

"Now, I must mention something. The police came round from Bristol, asking me about Jason. Remember him?"

Lucy coloured. She tried not to retch.

"I thought so." Daniel topped up his whisky and gave her another measure. "Look, it was clear from their questions that they suspect you of his murder."

Lucy caught her breath. That detective, Neil, had seemed hostile, but he hadn't accused her of the crime outright.

Daniel's solemn eyes fixed hers. "Did you do it, sis?"

"No." She shrank back into the sofa, breaking eye contact.

"Are you sure? Jason treated you shabbily." Daniel frowned. "We both know you've had mental health issues. Were you taking anything that night that made you forget? Even self-medicating with cannabis?"

She stuttered. "I didn't do drugs. There was just that one time, when Sarah brought space cakes round. I wasn't aware—"

"You pinched Mum and Dad's booze. I can see it in my mind, clear as day. You, out of your tiny little head. Girls will be girls, I said to Mum." Daniel smirked. "She didn't appreciate it at all. Still, if I'm honest, you were a nightmare as a teenager. You must admit that, at least."

"Possibly." Lucy hung her head, her cheeks seeming to burn hotter than the fire.

"Then are you positive there's nothing else you'd rather you hadn't done? If you dig deep, maybe you'll find it. Suppressed memories are a thing."

A strident buzzer sounded. A smart green and gold van had parked in the street outside. As Lucy watched, a raven-haired woman unloaded a rail of dark, flowing clothes. She was strikingly pretty and slim, a shape Lucy could only achieve by starving herself.

"Ah, Amanda has arrived with your gorgeous glad rags. You've been saved by the bell, sis." Daniel made for the door. He caught her eye again, holding her gaze through sheer force of personality. "Look, I may have suspicions but I'll say nothing to the police. I won't even say a word to Dad. We shouldn't worry him by mentioning Brett either."

"What about Harry?" she protested. "Can't you ask Brett where he is?"

"Melted down already, no doubt. I'll do my best. If I can't get that statue back, I'll find Mum another like it. You can sneak it into her lounge and she won't have the faintest idea." Daniel put a finger to his lips. "We should look out for each other, you and me. Blood is thicker than water. Remember that."

CHAPTER 22

LUCY

Like a monster in a dark tunnel, Zara blocked Lucy's path.

"Hello, Lucy, how are you?" Zara's eyes, enhanced by smoky make-up, were as sharp as her fringe.

Lucy obliged with the shortest possible answer. "Fine," she lied. Somehow, she functioned. She had returned from Richmond, cooked dinner for Sebastian, slept, woken, breakfasted, and taken the dog out. So far, she'd made it to Christchurch Green without collapsing in a sobbing heap. Who was fine, though, when they were suspected of murder? Who could feel fine when they'd witnessed the aftermath of a bloody fight? Worse, fears for her mother's future loomed like thunderclouds in the background.

The dog yanked at her leash. Lucy waited for Zara to ask about Jennifer, hoping for a swift escape afterwards.

"Still minding Sasha, I see," Zara observed. She must have forgotten Jennifer even existed.

Lucy nodded. The dog stopped pulling and nuzzled Zara's scarlet-tipped fingers, evidently wishing to be stroked.

Zara took no notice. "I see they've identified the dead man," she said in a conspiratorial whisper. "Jason Jordan from Dr Sweet."

"He was called Jason Jardine." Lucy blushed. She didn't want to talk about Jason to anyone, and if she ever changed her mind, Zara would be bottom of the list.

"Did you know him? The band used to practise in your cellar, didn't they?" Zara's face radiated curiosity.

"It wasn't exactly our cellar." Lucy twisted the leash around her wrists.

Luckily, Sasha took it as a call to action. With a yelp, the animal tried to slip through Zara's legs.

Lucy pulled the dog back, relieved at the excuse to dodge more questions. "I'm so sorry. Sasha always has a walk at ten, and we're fifteen minutes late." She shrugged, as if to say her hands were tied, and allowed the animal to drag her away.

Sasha set off at a steady pace until she spotted a squirrel. The dog hurtled towards it, Lucy clinging on to the lead and nearly tripping in the process.

Like quicksilver, the squirrel flashed up a tree trunk. Howling mournfully, Sasha stared at the branches above.

Marilyn, laden with supermarket bags, huffed and puffed across the green. It seemed there was no way to avoid company.

"Squirrels don't want to be friends?" Marilyn rearranged her bags to pet the animal. She sneezed. "I really shouldn't go near this dog with my allergies, but she's irresistible. Did I see Zara giving you the third degree, by the way?"

"You did," Lucy admitted.

"She's concerned about your mum, I expect, as we all are," Marilyn said.

"No." Lucy bit her lip. "She wanted to talk about Dr Sweet."

Marilyn's face fell. "I'll have a word with her. I'm sure she doesn't mean any harm, but she can't resist gossip, can she? At first, she was upset about the skeleton. Now she knows it was a celebrity, she's delighted. She'll be asking for a plaque next to her front door, I expect. Of course, it should be number 13's front door, shouldn't it?"

"That vault under the garden isn't ours. There might be a narrow tunnel from our own cellar, but it isn't safe to use." Lucy squirmed. Did Marilyn, too, think she'd killed Jason? If only she knew what she'd done when she last saw him. Then again, did she really want to remember? It was possibly for the best that she'd blotted out the memory with alcohol.

Marilyn's gaze was kind. "I meant because Daniel lived in your house once. He's such a superstar. Look, tell your dad not to worry about the cellar's ownership. It's under the council's land and they've taken responsibility. I have it on good authority."

"Brian?"

"Who else?" Marilyn patted her arm. "Don't fret about your mum, Lucy. She'll be patched up and back home before you know it. And don't let yourself get stressed about Zara either. Invent an errand when you next see her. You don't have to talk to anyone you don't wish to." With a sympathetic wink, she went on her way.

Lucy pondered on Marilyn's words. She preferred to steer clear of others, but the dog made it difficult. Sasha wanted to befriend all humans and animals they passed. It was easiest to take the line of least resistance and make small talk. To her surprise, it required her to concentrate so hard that she was distracted from her fears. By the time

Lucy had negotiated the Zig Zag and returned home, she had chatted to half a dozen folk. She astounded herself with a polite greeting to a journalist outside the central garden.

"Did you know Jason Jardine?" he asked, as the dog licked his fingers.

"No," Lucy lied, pulling Sasha away and chiding herself for dropping her guard.

Back inside, Lucy made tea for herself and coffee for her father. Although it was a Saturday morning, Sebastian was reading journals in his study. He had to catch up on work now he spent so much time at the hospital. Lucy felt a twinge of guilt. All she had from Daniel was a tentative commitment to see Jennifer. She should have pressed him further.

Sasha, energy spent, lay peaceably at Sebastian's feet. Her eyes briefly flicked open when Lucy arrived with the cafetière.

"She likes you," Lucy said.

"Told you. She recognises an alpha male." Sebastian's expression was smug. "What are your plans for the afternoon? I'm having a snifter at the Clifton Club, and then I'll see Jen."

"I've been asked to babysit. You know the couple at number 8? Their eldest is singing in a choir, and they want me to mind Freya. The little girl." She had considered cancelling, but walking the dog had shown her the importance of staying busy. A small child would need her full attention, and she wouldn't have space in her mind for worries.

"Are you sure?" Sebastian asked. "You haven't looked after children before."

"I did babysit once." Admittedly, it had been a long time ago. It hadn't ended well, either, but that was hardly Lucy's fault.

"I suppose it's all right. Just phone me if you need me, though, okay?" Sebastian looked less than thrilled at the prospect.

Lucy nodded, although she had no intention of calling him if her childcare went awry. Marilyn, who had recommended her to the new neighbours, was the obvious choice. Sebastian hadn't changed a nappy in his life. Nor had Jennifer when Daniel was a baby. In Singapore, there had been a nanny and maids. The return to England, at Sebastian's insistence, must have been a big upheaval. The house in Jackson Crescent was large enough to accommodate servants, but Sebastian's salary didn't stretch that far.

Just for once, the hidden chocolate stayed untouched. After her father left to join his friends, Lucy ate a ham sandwich without butter, settled the dog and went out. Blanking the journalist, she walked along the path to number 8.

She found the household in turmoil. Freya's mother had just been informed that the children's choir would perform in fancy dress. She was busy making her son a last-minute outfit. Her husband, a bearded entrepreneur who looked like a hipster clothing model, told Lucy this while she stood outside the door.

"We'll do the house tour first," he announced. "Freya is having a nap. Watch where you walk because the children haven't tidied up their toys yet."

It was wise advice. His home was an obstacle course, with spiky plastic objects strewn across the floor at random. Jennifer would never have allowed it at number 13. Lucy picked her way over the hazards as she visited the living room, playroom and kitchen. She was offered biscuits, and declined.

"All you ladies are watching your weight after Christmas," her guide observed.

Lucy didn't reply. She had a sudden desire to gag him with chocolate bourbons and stuff the rest of the packet into her own mouth. Shuddering, she allowed herself to be led to Freya's princess-themed bedroom.

There, long blonde hair spread around her like a halo, was the prettiest child Lucy had ever seen. Two-year-old Freya resembled an angel lying on a pink cloud.

Her father stroked her forehead tenderly. "Wake up, dear."

The child stretched and yawned. Her blue eyes flicked open, regarding Lucy with alarm.

At least she hadn't screamed. That was a good sign.

"Freya, dear," her father said, "this is Lucy. She's going to play with you this afternoon and take you for a haircut."

Lucy gawped at him. "Haircut?"

He seemed aghast. "Shoot. Didn't Laura mention it? I'm afraid it's been in the diary forever, and we can't rearrange. These appointments are like hen's teeth."

"We have a stylist who comes to our house," Lucy suggested.

He stared at her mop. "I don't think so."

That was harsh. Lucy wished she'd explained she simply had split ends chopped off. Jennifer's regular cut and colour displayed their hairdresser's talents much better.

It was plain he wouldn't change his mind. "So, she's booked in at three," he said. "We'd be terribly, terribly grateful."

His wife dashed into the room, a giant snowflake by her side. "Tom! Oscar and I are good to go. Are you ready?"

Laura was tall and thin, her clothes flattering and her posture perfect. Her poise gave the impression of a woman who could do anything and believed the world would help her do it. Lucy's school would have been proud of her.

With a start, Lucy realised they were around the same age.

Tom smiled at his wife. "Laura, you need to tell Lucy where to take Freya."

"Oh, didn't I say?" Laura turned wide, kohl-rimmed eyes to Lucy. "It's Hannah at Cutting Edge in the city centre. You can drive, can't you? Freya's stroller is a complete pain on the bus."

Lucy had the sensation of an abyss opening at her feet. "I'm afraid I can't."

"Didn't I see you in that massive BMW Tourer? It must have been your dad. Well, never mind." Laura unzipped her cowhide handbag with a self-satisfied smile. "Here's fifty quid. You'll need some of it for Hannah anyhow. Take taxis and get receipts for everything."

"So that's all sorted." Tom kissed his daughter's cheek. "Bye, dear. Ice cream when we come back, okay? Ciao, Lucy."

They departed in a buzz of noise and busyness. Downstairs, the front door slammed.

Freya burst into tears. "Want Mama."

Lucy thought ruefully of the bourbons. "She's coming back. How about a biscuit? Then we can play with your dolls."

The little girl's tears dried up at once. "Yeth."

Lucy guided Freya to the basement kitchen, taking care to ensure the toddler didn't trip on the stairs. The bourbons were gratefully received. With her new best friend, Lucy spent a happy thirty minutes feeding crumbs to Freya's dolls.

"Now we'll go to the centre of town, where all the big shops are. A taxi will come along to whisk us away. That'll be fun, won't it?" Listening to herself, Lucy was almost persuaded that it would be a fine adventure. It sounded more pleasurable than her trip to a nightmare in Richmond.

Freya's rosebud lip trembled. "Want thtroller."

"Well, I guess we could do that." She hadn't booked the taxi yet and there was enough time for the two mile walk to the city centre. It would have seemed impossible a month ago. Sasha had made a huge difference to Lucy's fitness.

Lucy dressed Freya in outdoor clothes and helped her into the stroller. As she manoeuvred it over the threshold, using the same techniques she'd applied to Jennifer's wheelchair, she wavered. She'd have to push Freya all the way. Still, it was downhill, so how hard could it be?

Now Lucy discovered that strangers adored small children as much as dogs. She had hardly set foot outside Jackson Crescent before a passer-by complimented her on Freya's beauty. Others mistook Lucy for Freya's mother and pointed out similarities in nose shape and hair colour. Lucy basked in reflected glory, enjoying it so much that she didn't admit the truth.

The city centre was bustling, although not as cramped as the jam-packed platforms of Bristol Temple Meads. It didn't feel as stressful. The stroller acted as an informal battering ram, crowds parting before it. She was on a high when she arrived at the charming, glass-roofed arcade. Next to a modern mall, it hosted cute boutiques rather than chain stores. Lucy looked around for the hair salon and caught a glimpse of her reflection in a window. She scarcely recognised this pretty, carefree young woman. Flicking her hair back, she simpered with sheer delight. Then she noticed the mirrored image of a familiar face behind her. This one wasn't smiling.

CHAPTER 23

NEIL

Neil had rarely been so angry in his life. The air seemed infused with tension, like the still moment before an electrical storm.

Gemma immediately sensed it. She grasped his arm. "What's wrong?"

He uncurled his clenched fists, pointing a finger. "That woman should not be in charge of a child."

Gemma looked baffled. "I don't see the problem. They're completely at ease with each other."

Neil simmered. "You don't understand what she's capable of. And I'm not allowed to tell you. But I'm not letting it go."

"Are you on duty?" Gemma asked.

"No, but it doesn't matter." Neil squinted at the small girl in the stroller. She didn't resemble Lucy Freeman, but that proved nothing. Babies were podgy little people who all looked the same, unless, as with Lucas, you knew them well. There hadn't been any sign of a child at 13 Jackson Crescent and nobody had mentioned one. He wished he'd asked more questions.

Self-absorbed as ever, Lucy was ignoring the tot and admiring her reflection in a shop window. The kid glanced in his direction and began to wail. That decided him. Neil shook his hand free. He stepped towards the pair.

Lucy turned around, her smile fading.

"How come you're looking after a child? Is she yours?" He almost spat the words out.

Lucy clutched the stroller tightly. "No. Freya is a friend's daughter, and I'm taking her to the hairdresser. Aren't I, honeybun? You need it cut." She stroked the little girl's locks.

Freya stopped crying. Her black patent-shod feet kicked out at him. Lucy was clearly incapable of controlling the child.

"Can you give me your friend's name and address, please?" Neil asked.

Lucy gaped at him, shrinking back and pressing herself against the glass as if hoping it would swallow her. "Why do you want to know?"

Neil wished he could tell them never to let Lucy near their daughter again, that she was a murderess who forced children to take drugs. Unfortunately, he'd be risking his career. He had no proof. Jackson Crescent residents were the sort of people who knew their rights, and they enjoyed gossiping. Lucy's father would get to hear about it if Neil made unsubstantiated accusations about his daughter. A high-flying academic wouldn't let it go; he'd lodge a complaint.

"Listen," he whispered, so Gemma wouldn't hear, "I do not want any harm to come to that child. In fact, I'll be checking up to make sure it doesn't. Now give me their contact details, please."

"You've no right," Lucy stammered.

She quivered, her teeth chattering. Was she taking drugs even now? Neil peered into her eyes. They seemed entirely normal.

The child said, "Naughty man," in tones of profound disgust.

"Hush, Freya." In soothing the child, Lucy appeared to collect herself. She said, "Tom and Laura Lewin. They live at number 8."

"Jackson Crescent?"

"Yes."

"Thank you." Taking a deep breath, Neil added. "Just go to the hairdresser, then take that child home."

Lucy nodded. Without a word, she wheeled the stroller to a hair salon two doors away. Neil watched her being greeted and seated. A smaller chair was produced for the toddler. They were obviously expected.

He couldn't keep staring at them forever. As a young woman began combing and snipping the infant's hair, he risked a sidelong glance at Gemma. She seemed subdued and puzzled. The trip to the arcade, to show her independent shops and a craft jeweller's, had been ruined by Lucy Freeman.

"I'm sorry," he said. "Work intrudes sometimes."

Gemma squeezed his hand. "Don't worry. I wouldn't expect any less of you. You've got to protect the public."

"Right." At her touch, tension began to drain from his limbs. He smiled at her.

Gemma took a good look at the trio in the salon: the infant sitting quietly, the cutter chatting to her and the fair-haired woman gazing at them fondly. "What a sweet little girl," she said. "And that lady who's with her – it's not the mother, is it? – she's lovely. A very caring person."

Why would she speak of Lucy so warmly? He'd imagined that Gemma had sound judgement, that she was intuitive about people's natures. When they'd first met at her parents' B&B, she'd spotted quickly enough that Uncle Roy was a moron. She made an unlikely champion for Lucy Freeman.

He shook his head. "Appearances can be deceptive, I'm afraid."

"Of course," Gemma agreed. "But I was struck by a sensation of kindness as soon as I saw her. She has a loving heart."

"That's possible," Neil conceded grudgingly. "But she's completely untrustworthy. Maybe she has mental health issues. I have proof that she lied to me in my investigations. And she gave me space cakes as a child."

Gemma stared at him. "Really?"

"Yes, really. I was only four years old. My mother asked Lucy to babysit me and she fed me hash brownies."

"Do you think she meant to?" Gemma asked.

"How could it have been an accident? Look at her now, in charge of that little kiddie. I don't know what to do."

Gemma's wise green eyes fixed his. "Why not try believing her?"

CHAPTER 24

LUCY

An aroma of roast chicken wafted through the kitchen. Sasha was Lucy's constant shadow again, having forsaken alpha male Sebastian to sniff hopefully at the oven. Lucy patted the dog's head. Her heart felt dull and leaden, as if it would sink all the way down to her feet and never rise again. Margaret Forsyth was coming back.

What would she do without the Samoyed? Sasha's friendly presence distracted Lucy from her constant worries, the greatest of which was her mother's health. The hospital stay had compromised Jennifer's already limited mobility. She would be transferring to a rehabilitation unit. Sebastian seemed to think she would recover and be sent home to continue as before. Lucy doubted it. Jennifer's condition meant she was already living on borrowed time. One day, she would be gone forever, and Lucy would be forced to confront the question she'd been avoiding: what was her purpose in life?

Biting her lip, she checked on the crispy potatoes and Mediterranean-style vegetables in the oven. In ten minutes, they would be done. She laid three of the good Wedgwood plates out on the table, covered with a snowy cloth in Margaret's honour. Their neighbour would join them for Sunday lunch before Lucy and Sebastian visited Jennifer in hospital. Lucy switched on Radio 3, hoping to catch a concert of early Renaissance music.

Six short beeps announced the top of the hour. A news bulletin began. Lucy listened with half an ear, removing the chicken from the oven and setting it on an oval platter to rest. She chose another piece of Wedgwood on which to serve it. Setting gravy to simmer, she jumped at the words, "…also known as Count Brett Hollande. Mr Smith, who had recently been released on licence, was sentenced to life for murder and blackmail over four decades ago. He had links with the Bristol area, where he was living in a probation hostel. A dog walker found his body in a ditch just off the A3 in Surrey, and police—"

The doorbell sounded.

"Can you get that, Lucy?" Sebastian yelled from his study. "I'm on the phone."

The newsman was already talking about something else. Hands trembling as she removed the gravy saucepan from the hob, Lucy dashed upstairs.

Margaret Forsyth, elegant as ever in a velvet cape and smart trousers, stood clutching a bottle of wine. "It's good to be back in the crescent. So kind of Sebastian to arrange a warm welcome at this troubling time. And I assume you're our chef, Lucy?"

"Do come in." Lucy set her lips into a smile-shaped grimace. She ushered her neighbour into the hall and took her cape. Underneath, Margaret wore a gold silk blouse that accentuated the light tan colour of her skin. Style came easily if you were slim like her or rich like Daniel. Lucy remembered how her bloodied clothes had been so swiftly replaced with flattering new garments. There was no evidence linking her to the dead Brett. Presumably, nothing connected Daniel with the deceased man either. How had Brett's body ended up in a ditch? Was it simply that, as a murderer and blackmailer, he had made enemies?

"Oh dear," Margaret said. "Life in Jackson Crescent has been eventful lately. Have you had time to practise your singing?"

Lucy chose to be vague. "Not exactly. We were too worried about Mum."

"Sebastian told me everything."

Lucy doubted it. Sebastian didn't know half of her troubles. She nodded, the fake smile firmly in place.

Margaret's expression was sympathetic, for all that she and Jennifer had not been bosom buddies. "How awful for you all. When I'm settled, I'll pop round to the hospital with flowers for her. But talking of getting organised, I'm afraid I'm going to ask another favour of you and your father."

A loud crash from the basement interrupted the conversation.

"Where is Sasha?" Margaret asked.

They exchanged shocked glances.

Lucy had been so wrapped up in the news story, it hadn't occurred to her that the dog usually bounded upstairs with her to the front door. Why had Sasha stayed in the kitchen? "The chicken," she cried in dismay, dashing down the stairwell. It had been on the worktop, which she'd expected to be out of the dog's reach. Evidently, she'd been wrong.

Wagging her tail, Sasha was eyeing the roast bird, which lay on the floor with its platter on top of it. By a small miracle, the crockery was unbroken.

"I got here just in time," Sebastian said, one hand on the dog's collar and the other holding a phone.

"Bad dog," Margaret said. "Lucy, if you just throw away the chicken skin, I'm sure we can eat the rest."

Sasha looked sheepish as Lucy picked up the dish.

Sebastian put down his phone. "It's hard to stay cross with Sasha for long. Please sit down, Margaret. How kind of you to bring wine. Let me pour you a glass."

"Thank you, just a small one. I'm terribly sorry, by the way, but I've discovered an awful water leak in my flat—"

Before Margaret could speak further, Sebastian said, "Oh dear. Would you like us to take care of Sasha until you've got it sorted?"

"That would be enormously sweet of you, Sebastian. Yes, please."

The lead weight pressing on Lucy's heart began to lift.

"Your dog has won us over, despite her bad habits." Sebastian patted Sasha's head.

"She will be getting spoiled. Don't give her the skin, Lucy." Margaret caught the dog's eye. "No scraps for you after that performance."

Sasha appeared to understand. She slunk into a corner.

Lucy placed the food in the centre of the table while Sebastian filled their glasses. At last, she sat down and started to eat. She tried to banish the shock of the radio news to a corner of her mind, to compartmentalise, as Sebastian seemed able to do. The wine might help. It was an Australian chardonnay: dry, yet fruity. She downed it quickly.

"I didn't think you were a big drinker, Lucy," Margaret commented. She picked up the bottle to pour some more.

"No thanks, I'm not." Lucy covered her glass with her palm. "It's so delicious, I didn't realise how much I'd had." Already a warm glow was stealing over her. Her cares began to vanish.

She rarely shared a meal with others. Lucy felt a wave of nostalgia for the family meals of her childhood. Daniel had teased her and Jennifer had inspected Lucy's portions too closely, but at least they had all been together. They couldn't know how time would take Daniel far away from

Bristol, ravage Jennifer's health and turn Lucy's dreams into failure. Only Sebastian seemed unchanged, with his books and lectures and his adoration for his wife. Now, he gave Margaret an exhaustive account of Jennifer's recent illness.

"…and she can't really eat properly in the hospital," he finished. "Both Lucy and I have been feeding her on our visits."

That was news to Lucy. She'd been taking yogurt and other soft food to build her mother's strength, carefully spooning morsels into Jennifer's mouth, but she hadn't realised her father had done the same. He must have bought provisions in the hospital shops.

"Your home cooking will cheer her up," Margaret said. "This is exceedingly tasty. My daughter is a vegetarian, so it's a treat to eat meat again."

"And how is she? Better, I hope," Lucy asked. With a glass of wine inside her, conversation was less awkward.

"She's full of energy. The baby didn't catch flu from her, luckily." Margaret laughed. "You will be amused by this. I love a book at bedtime and my daughter has nothing to read except romance novels. I became quite an addict."

293

"Well, I think we have shelves full of them," Sebastian said, "and you'd be welcome to take them away. They're Jen's, but she listens to audiobooks now."

Lucy shot him a puzzled glance. "I don't remember seeing any love stories."

"Your mother filled a bookcase in my bedroom. I guess you didn't notice because they're not your sort of book. You prefer swords and sorcery, don't you, Lucy?"

Lucy nodded. She had merely the sketchiest knowledge of Sebastian's bedroom, because she never ventured there. Her parents had shared it until Jennifer could no longer navigate stairs. Sebastian hadn't changed anything, maintaining it as a shrine to his wife, or at least to the wife Jennifer had once been. It was surprising that he wanted to dispose of her books. Perhaps he realised how much she was declining.

"I'd happily take them off your hands," Margaret offered.

"Great. Lucy, why don't you pop upstairs while I serve pudding?" Sebastian suggested.

The dessert, a low calorie chocolate ice cream, required little culinary skill on his part. Lucy left him to scoop it into dishes. She took a carrier bag to the first floor, approaching Sebastian's bedroom hesitantly. Their cleaner kept the room spotless, but the faint smell of lavender polish added to the air of a time warp.

Her gaze was drawn to the diary on the mahogany dressing table. It was an expensive make, covered in a peacock feather design with gold embossing. She reached for it, stroking the cover at first. Timorously, she flipped it open with one finger, feeling the smooth cream paper, seeing a date in 2013. Jennifer's handwriting was already starting to deteriorate then, just as her speech had initially slurred.

Lucy read the words, 'GP confirmed Parkinsons. Not a death sentence, he says. Feels like it.'.

An icy shiver ran through her. Whatever her own problems, even if she really was guilty of murder and would spend the rest of her life behind bars, nothing could be worse than Jennifer's imprisonment in a body that no longer functioned.

The last entry, dated the twentieth of July 2013, was barely legible.

"Lucy! Pudding is served. Any luck?" Sebastian yelled. He must be standing at the foot of the stairwell.

"Coming," she shouted back.

Jennifer's words had struck a chord. Although Lucy couldn't ask her mother what happened at the turn of the millennium, she could interrogate the journals. Jennifer surely hadn't been involved in Jason's murder, but there might be clues within her written memories, pointers to Lucy's innocence. Lucy resolved to return later to find them.

Meanwhile, she turned her attention to the bookcase, another carved mahogany piece. Picking up a pair of Maeve Binchy paperbacks from the top shelf, she spotted a splash of crimson behind them.

It was a glossy red diary. Lucy gasped, her heart thumping. She removed more novels and knew she'd struck gold. Jennifer had hidden her journals here: books bound like works of art with pictures of butterflies, flowers, and trees. Quickly, Lucy flicked each one open to look for dates.

At last, she found the year 2000. She read, 'We agreed we'd go to France together. I can pass for J if I wear his hat.'

Lucy nearly dropped the diary. She turned the page, eager to read more, yet afraid of what she would see.

Sebastian's footsteps pounded on the stairs. Desperately, Lucy stacked Jennifer's notebooks on the shelf, filling the bag with the hefty Maeve Binchy volumes.

"Are you all right?" Sebastian looked concerned. "I didn't think it would take you so long."

"Sorry, I couldn't fit them all in the carrier. There are too many."

Sebastian peered at the bookcase. "I see what you mean. Let's take the rest down after we've eaten. That ice cream is going to melt soon."

He was being extraordinarily practical. Lucy suspected Margaret had sent him to fetch her. She followed him back to the kitchen.

"Margaret, take a look," Sebastian urged, motioning to Lucy to give the bag to their neighbour.

"Let's tuck in first." Margaret beamed at them. "Sin-free chocolate. How extraordinary. It's too good to be true."

The frozen dessert was unexpectedly delectable. Lucy still thought longingly of her hidden treats in the cupboard. She busied herself serving coffee while Margaret inspected the books.

"Any good?" Sebastian asked.

Margaret's tone was rueful. "These are family sagas, aren't they? I'm afraid my romance story addiction doesn't stretch that far. I'm terribly sorry to have put you to the trouble."

"It's no trouble at all," Sebastian said. It was clear he had no idea of the difference. "We'll take these books to a charity shop. I can use the space upstairs for my philosophy texts."

"You couldn't perhaps declutter your own library too?" Margaret winked at Lucy.

Sebastian spluttered into his coffee.

Later, as Lucy loaded the dishwasher with lunchtime crockery, she pondered on Sebastian's question to her. He had asked if she was all right, when he only really cared about making room for his academic books. Sebastian hadn't expected an answer, and she hadn't insisted on telling him. How could she be all right when she stood accused of murder and might even be guilty?

Could she have murdered Jason in cold blood? She didn't remember being angry during their last encounter, just ashamed and upset. Her memories were hazy thanks to the whisky, hastily gulped while she pinched her nose. Had guilt, rather than misery, driven her to the bottle? Her pets had died, although she loved them. Like theirs, Jason's death might have been accidental, but ultimately her responsibility.

The detective, Neil, thought she'd done it. That was obvious from the way he'd approached her in the arcade. He'd told Daniel he suspected her and even her beloved brother didn't believe in her innocence. Yet Daniel knew more than he'd said. He had helped Jennifer cover it up. They must have gone to France together, Jennifer disguising herself as Jason. Lucy supposed that, with her hair hidden beneath the hat and some dark foundation cream, Jennifer could have passed for a man. Obviously, she had. The ploy had succeeded, as evidenced by all the media coverage of Jason disappearing in France. He hadn't gone to France at all.

Who had killed him, then? Surely not Daniel? Jason was his best friend. Besides, Dr Sweet was everything to her brother, and the band depended on Jason for their songs. With Jason out of the picture, it was touch and go whether Dr Sweet would survive. If Alfie Bucks hadn't arrived on the scene, they might have folded.

Had Jennifer done it? Lucy couldn't imagine her mother capable of murder. Then again, Jennifer was prone to outbursts. There had been the incident with the brownies, when Lucy had embarrassed Jennifer in front of her new friend. Her mother's rage had flared like a firework. For a terrifying moment, Lucy had believed Jennifer would throttle her. Her anger only subsided when Daniel explained that Sarah had supplied the space cakes.

Jennifer had banned Sarah from the house. Jason was cooling towards her anyway, Daniel had said at the time. He was indifferent to Sarah's absence or presence. She was little more than a groupie.

Incredibly, Jennifer had believed Daniel's assurance that the doped cakes were a one-off event and the band had never done drugs otherwise. In reality, they had smoked cannabis in the cellar both before and afterwards. Lucy didn't touch it. She was no drinker either. It meant the whisky had hit her like a sledgehammer. Even if she'd murdered Jason, she was in no fit state to lay a false trail.

Had Daniel done that for her? He was a mother's boy, but surely he'd have jibbed at helping Jennifer if she'd perpetrated a gruesome crime. He would have gone through with it for

Lucy, though. When she needed Daniel, when it really counted, he was there. They weren't as close as they'd been as children, but he'd warned her about Neil Slater's suspicions. Then, he'd been so considerate and replaced her ruined clothes. Back in October 2000, he could and would have used his charm to persuade Jennifer to help. Her mother and brother must have hidden the body and carried out the elaborate charade for Lucy's sake.

It would explain why Daniel so rarely came home. He must have been grief-stricken by his best friend's traumatic death. It would account for Jennifer's coldness towards her daughter, too. Lucy shifted uneasily as she considered Jennifer's attitude towards her. She couldn't recall a single episode of kindness or warmth, even before the trip to France. Tears stung her eyes.

Sasha was licking a bowl which, contrary to Margaret's instructions, had contained chicken scraps. The dog stood up and padded across to Lucy, nuzzling her hand.

Lucy took the hint and tickled Sasha's ears. The animal's presence soothed her. Eventually, she stopped crying.

Jennifer's diaries held the key. Lucy had turned the page forward, when she should have been looking back to see what happened in the cellar. She crept upstairs, feeling like a thief, heart hammering in her chest.

The bookcase was empty.

Peering in from the bedroom's threshold, Lucy reeled. As before, when she recalled her last contact with Jason, she began to doubt the truth of her own senses. Tentatively, she stepped into the room and ran a finger across the shelves. There was dust at the back, where a cleaner couldn't reach without moving books. Where had they gone?

She heard the front door open downstairs and Sasha's joyful greeting to the arrival. Scurrying down, she saw Sebastian in the hall, an empty rucksack flapping around him.

"I've started decluttering," he announced with pride.

"Mum's books?"

"Quite so. The Oxfam shop in Clifton Village is open on Sundays, so I thought I'd strike while the iron was hot. Now I'm going to move a few texts from my study. Just the popular philosophy, for bedtime reading."

It wasn't a good time to mention that Sebastian's idea of bedtime reading didn't chime with hers. "What about her diaries?" Lucy asked.

Sebastian looked bewildered. "I didn't notice any."

Lucy grabbed a coat. "They were with the romance stories. I'll get them back."

"But it's visiting time. We should be seeing your mother."

"Sorry, Dad. You go ahead. I'll join you later." She helped herself to a set of keys and slouched out, hands in pockets.

She had Daniel and Amanda to thank for her coat. The hooded, flowing garment, a charcoal cashmere lined with blue silk, was the prettiest item of clothing she owned. As she hurried to the local Oxfam bookshop, Zara stopped her to ask if she was losing weight.

The shop wasn't busy. A bored young man, whippet-thin and sporting a goatee beard, manned the till on the off chance that the sole browser would make a purchase.

"Excuse me." Lucy parked herself in front of goatee man. "My father brought some novels in earlier, but he made a mistake and included a load of diaries too. They'd been written in, so obviously you can't sell them."

"That's no problem." He had a nasal whine. "Anything we can't sell, we send for recycling."

"Well, we'd quite like them back." That was an understatement, of course. "They're of sentimental value."

He glanced at the area around the till. "All donations are in the stockroom now. If I could help, I would, but I can't go there and look. You can see I'm on my own."

"Could you find them later, please?" Lucy stood tall, surprised by her own assertiveness. It was amazing how desperation changed your behaviour.

Goatee man sucked his teeth. "No promises. But sure, I'll see what I can do. Can you describe them for me?"

"There are at least half a dozen. About this size." Lucy picked up a paperback. "One of the covers is cream, with pink butterflies." That was the book she yearned most of all to find. She concentrated hard to visualise the others, conveying a sense of them as best she could. Finally, she told him they had been brought in with a large quantity of Maeve Binchy novels.

He took her telephone number. Thanking him profusely, she hoped he would find them. Even more, she hoped he wouldn't read them. If he did, what terrible truths would he uncover?

CHAPTER 25

NEIL

Neil reached ten thousand steps and switched off the cross trainer. He could murder a coffee and didn't mind telling Ab.

"You nearly done, boss?"

Ab, pounding the pedals on an exercise bike, flashed a toothy white grin. "Two minutes."

Neil headed for a power shower. Usually, the gym session would see him refreshed and energised. It marked his transition from home life to the working day. This Monday morning, both were bleeding into each other, and he didn't like it. After the encounter with Lucy Freeman, there was no chance of steering Gemma to a jewellery workshop and coaxing her into choosing a ring. She had insisted on stopping for a coffee, admittedly a superb three-shot Americano in a café he wouldn't have thought to frequent. They had eaten gluten-free cake while she quizzed him about his thoughts on Lucy. He had spoken as freely as the law allowed him to. Gemma had listened, squeezing his hand. His emotions, she said, were all about Neil Slater and not about the case.

He acknowledged a grain of truth in Gemma's words, but Lucy remained his prime suspect. It irked him that, as a small cog in a big wheel, he couldn't angle the investigation towards her.

The weekend hadn't been entirely wasted, of course. He had walked with Gemma in the green spaces that curled around the heart of Bristol: elegant Brandon Hill and the vast, sweeping Downs. She now realised trees grew within the city. They had strolled along gentrified North Street, not far from the shared house he had hastily cleaned as soon as his flatmates left. Although hardly Glastonbury, the area boasted independent shops and a gastropub which welcomed vegans.

He might tempt her to the city yet, but it would take time. If all else failed, he'd have to adopt a plant-based diet and transfer to the Somerset Levels. Gloomily, Neil imagined a future where the most exciting event of his day would be giving Ethan Stokesley a speeding ticket.

He tried to let the hot water wash away his cares, then towelled himself vigorously. Ab was waiting in the changing rooms, clean, smart, and fragrant with the aftershave he'd received for Christmas.

"What took you so long?" Ab tapped his watch. Neil shrugged.

"Girl trouble?" Ab hazarded. "You should let your parents fix you up; it's easier."

His mother would undoubtedly like nothing more. Neil shuddered. "Let's get that caffeine," he suggested.

The gym had a small lounge, rarely patronised during the morning peak, although a few newspapers were left out. The coffee came from a machine, but it was palatable and cheap. Neil and Ab bought Americanos and sat by a glass screen overlooking the weights area.

Although the other seats were unoccupied, Ab still glanced around to ensure no-one overheard. "Op Indigo is becoming a bigger pain every day. There's the latest headache." He picked up one of the tabloids.

At first, Neil thought Pete Willoughby must have sold his story. Then he read, 'My sad love triangle' and saw a very old photograph of Sarah Stokesley in a bikini top and miniskirt.

"I suppose she needed money for her roof." It crossed Neil's mind that the commune couldn't have been growing marijuana unless they were very bad at it or smoked it all themselves. He'd expect it to fund a better lifestyle than Sarah enjoyed.

"Wait until SuperTed sees it." Ab's tone was grim. "As it is, he's breathing down my neck almost hourly. He emailed me at six this morning."

"Were you up?" Neil had been in the Land of Nod until quarter to seven, having learned to dress, scoff breakfast cereal and drive to the gym in under thirty minutes.

Ab laughed. "Yes, and I replied to let him know. I've got a baby daughter. Sleep is optional. I can't say why SuperTed is functional before first light, too. Maybe he's a vampire. Anyhow, between you and me, he's besotted with his new partner in Jackson Crescent. It gives him a particular interest in the case."

"As in, showing off to his girlfriend?" Neil smirked.

"I didn't say that." Ab's voice regained its equanimity. "In any event, I agree with you that the Freeman family merit further investigation. They knew Jason Jardine, he was found in a location to which only they had access, and they've lied about it. And given you drugs if your mother is to be believed."

"I wouldn't question her integrity." Neil grimaced.

Ab returned his frown. "No need for a sense of humour failure. As I've said before, she might have been mistaken. It doesn't affect my view of the action we should take. We don't have enough evidence to arrest Sebastian and Lucy Freeman on suspicion of murder. I'd like to bring them in for questioning, but I think we'd waste our time. They'll tell us nothing and we'll have to let them go. So, I want to search their house from top to bottom, including cellars. Let's see if they have other skeletons, real or metaphorical, stashed away."

Finally, Ab had listened. Neil felt a rush of adrenaline. "We'll need a warrant, surely, boss? If we're not making an arrest."

"SuperTed is arranging it," Ab said. "We'll discuss it further at the meeting in thirty minutes. Can I assume you're up for doing the search?"

"Count me in," Neil said.

CHAPTER 26

LUCY

Lucy woke with a headache. It intensified as she pulled on her clothes. Daniel had bought these garments, too. Amanda called them a jogging suit. That was a laugh. Women who reached for elasticated trousers and a loose top weren't the type to jog. The sky blue colour flattered her eyes, however, and she liked the deceptively slimming cut.

She winced at her throbbing temples. After taking paracetamol, she crept downstairs, listening for a hint that Sebastian was up and about. No clattering noises came from the bathroom, or yawns from his study. The house seemed unnaturally quiet. As long as he wasn't in the kitchen, her chocolate would remain a secret from him. She tiptoed there and fished it out of its hiding place for the first time in days.

The dog's liquid brown eyes regarded her reproachfully.

"I'm just having one square," she told the animal. "And I'd share, but it's bad for you." She filled Sasha's water and food bowls, adding a slice of raw bacon to the uninviting dried pellets. It didn't stop her feeling guilty. She made herself tea and reached for another piece of chocolate.

The Oxfam shop didn't open for another hour. Lucy attempted to tidy the kitchen cupboards, but found it hard to focus. She needed that diary. The little book with its pink butterflies held the proof of her innocence or guilt. The more she chewed the facts over in her head, the more fearful she became. How would she deal with the truth?

Daniel was in the clear. He and his bandmates relied on Jason for Dr Sweet's existence. Sebastian had no motive either. That left only two possibilities. Had Jennifer's hatred for Jason flared into fury? Lucy had loved him, or so she'd thought. Even so, had she lashed out when he spurned her?

There was a ping from the phone in her pocket. Lucy saw she'd received a text from Daniel: "Ring me ASAP, sis."

Despite the painkillers, her headache returned. She scrolled to his number.

"Sis?" He sounded as stressed as she felt. "Why does Dad want to see me?"

"Sorry, what do you mean?" Perhaps Sebastian had lost patience. It was about time his son visited Jennifer.

She heard Daniel gasp. Then he said, "Dad phoned earlier. Actually, I wasn't at my best. I hadn't been in bed long, you know? He demanded I came straight to Bristol."

"So you're on your way?" Lucy's delight bubbled into her voice.

"Yes, but what's it about? He was insistent. Said we needed to talk now, and he'd never speak to me again if I didn't come. I don't understand why he couldn't just have a conversation on the phone."

Lucy was silent. That didn't sound like Sebastian. Where was he, anyway? If he hadn't gone to the university, she would have expected him to turn up in the kitchen with an empty coffee mug.

"It's not as if I don't have my own problems," Daniel grumbled. "Sarah's done a kiss and tell. I'm going to sack my PR agents. They'd have stopped it if they did their jobs properly."

For a moment, Lucy tried to concentrate on her brother's troubles rather than her own. "I'm not an expert on PR, but shouldn't you be getting your agents to limit the damage? It's probably not the best time to sack them."

"You're right. Look, if anyone from the media comes round—"

She stared at the phone. What planet was he on? The media had camped out in Jackson Crescent for weeks. "I'll say 'no comment.'"

"Thanks, sis. She's alleged I broke up the band. You know that's a pack of lies. I kept it going, didn't I? Now Dr Sweet's diehard fans will be out for my blood. I'm wearing dark glasses in public until it dies down. Maybe I should grow a beard to disguise myself."

"Wait." She'd been accused of a much more heinous crime. Her sympathy was increasingly strained. "You mentioned a disguise? I read an old diary of Mum's."

There was a long pause before Daniel spoke again. "What did it say?"

"She pretended to be Jason. He didn't go to France with you, did he? It was her."

"Yes. She talked me into it." Daniel's chuckle had a bitter edge. "What else did you read?"

"Nothing. Dad took the journals to Oxfam by mistake. I'm trying to get them back. Don't you see? At last, I can find out how Jason died." As she finished, she regretted the stupidity of her remark. Daniel must already know the truth, or at least Jennifer's version of it.

"Sis, you really don't remember, do you? Mum told me you killed him. Let sleeping dogs lie."

Lucy nearly dropped the phone. Her heart pounded and waves of pain engulfed her head. "That's what the police think, Daniel. But I didn't. What can I do? I don't want to go to prison. Who will look after Mum when she's back home?" She couldn't face the even worse alternative, that Jennifer might not come back.

"Quite sure you didn't do it?" he asked gently.

How could she be sure? She didn't reply.

"Calm down. It will be all right as long as you hold your nerve." His voice was kind. "The police can't prove anything. They never will, provided they don't lay their hands on Mum's diary. You mustn't go searching for it. Just sit tight, and if the cops harass you any more, I'll pay for a good lawyer. Okay?"

"Okay." Like chocolate, her brother was there for her when it really mattered.

"See you later, sis. Got to go."

She set the phone down and snapped off another two squares. The dog, after sitting quietly at

Lucy's feet, began barking and running round the kitchen in circles.

"What's the matter, Sasha? Is it time for your walk?" For once, Lucy didn't feel up to the Zig Zag. Fresh air might help, though.

Sebastian stumbled into the kitchen. He looked drained, his eyes reddened and sunken. "Any chance of a coffee?"

"I'll make some." Before she could say more, Sasha jumped up at Sebastian, licking his hands.

Sebastian petted the dog. "Man's best friend." A tear trickled down his cheek.

Afraid she would spill it, Lucy stopped pouring boiling water into the cafetière. "What's wrong, Dad? It's Mum, isn't it?"

"Yes. Not the way you think. She's still in a stable condition in the heart ward."

"I just spoke to Daniel, Dad. He said he's coming here because you made him. What's going on?" She sat down, her legs wobbly. She'd never seen Sebastian cry before. Had Daniel told him she was a murderer?

Sebastian paced around the room. "I've got news I can't give him over the phone."

"Will you tell me?" Lucy folded her arms, hugging herself. Whatever he was about to divulge, it couldn't be good.

"Well," his expression was grave, "I realised I hadn't taken Jen's diaries to the Oxfam shop after all. In an absent-minded moment, I'd left them in my study."

Lucy's jaw dropped. He'd lied to her. Now he would say he'd read the journals and knew she was a killer. Would he give her a chance to escape before he told the police? Perhaps that was why he'd summoned Daniel, to help her get away. Sebastian had been talking about her mother, though. Had Jennifer taken Jason's life?

A flush rose over Sebastian's pale face. "I've never opened her diaries before, of course. They're private. But I thought if I took them to the hospital and read them with her, it would buck her up. I leafed through them to find happy passages to share. And I discovered I'm not Daniel's father."

Lucy dug her nails into her arms. Her chair rattled beneath her. She must be rocking in it.

"He was a man called Count Brett Hollande." Sebastian clenched his fists. "You told me he visited just before Jen became ill. I'd have

317

punched his lights out if I'd had the slightest inkling."

Lucy gaped at him. The revelation should have come as more of a shock, but she'd assumed a family link to Brett once she'd spotted his resemblance to Daniel. Sebastian's primeval desire for violence alarmed her more. Her mild-mannered father rarely exhibited even a hint of anger.

She guessed he didn't know that Brett was a criminal who had died in suspicious circumstances. This wasn't the time to mention it.

"You told me he stole Harry. I wish I'd believed you." Sebastian peered at Lucy's face. His voice softened. "You're so obviously my daughter. Jen deceived me about many things. About her background, her feelings towards me, and her affairs. But not about that."

Lucy flung her arms around him, noticing the tension in his shoulders and spine. "I love you, Dad. I'm sure Mum does too." She wasn't certain at all, but it seemed the right thing to say.

Her father howled. Deep, wracking sobs surged through his body as Lucy clung to him. Sasha whimpered beside them, finally adding a mournful wail.

Sebastian broke away and stroked the animal. "I wish we could keep this dog," he said. "I should have put my foot down when Jen wouldn't let you have one as a child. Admittedly, your track record wasn't brilliant, but your life might have been nicer if I'd stuck up for you more."

Lucy reddened. She could be a murderer. Sebastian shouldn't waste his affection on her. "I don't mind. You weren't the kind of dad who was around much." It didn't make him exceptional. Her schoolmates' fathers often had jobs that kept them away from their families, travelling to London or further afield. It was how they afforded the fees.

"She never cared about anyone except herself," Sebastian said slowly, as if learning a new truth. His voice cracked as he added, "There were so many signs I ignored. Daniel doesn't look like either Jen or me. His hair is so dark. I used to joke about it, tell her that he was a changeling. I thought nothing of it, or her nights out with friends in Singapore. I caught her out just once. Daniel was nearly ten by then, and she told me she was taking him to the zoo. By chance, I spotted him walking down the street with his nanny."

The furies had escaped from the box. Sebastian seemed impelled to tell her details she didn't wish to hear, and Lucy felt compelled to listen. Her head ached as the furies' cynical laughter buzzed around it.

His mouth twitched. "I used a private investigator then. It turned out I even knew the fellow she was seeing. He was another academic. Life and soul of the party. You know the sort?"

Lucy stayed quiet. She didn't live in a world where party animals courted beautiful women.

"Jen played me for a fool. She told me he'd been the only one. A night of passion resulting from too much wine. She claimed to be mortified when she sobered up. We agreed we'd have a baby to patch up our marriage. At least one good thing came out of it, then. You appeared in our lives."

Since her childhood, others had said Lucy looked like him beneath her plumpness. Still, how could he know for sure?

Sebastian answered her unspoken question. "Jen didn't pull any punches with her journals. She was completely frank. I read every single line—"

"All of them?" She held her breath.

Sebastian ignored the interruption. "—from the day we met to the day you were born. There were scores of infidelities. Hundreds. When I found out about that one man, she had a wake-up call. She feared I'd leave and take Daniel." He sighed, exhaling sour breath. His skin had a greenish cast, as if he was about to be sick. It was possible he already had been.

"Why didn't you read any more?" Lucy asked, her voice quivering.

"I'd seen as much as I could stand. And what I needed. I knew you were mine. Then I fell asleep at my desk." He stretched his limbs. "Everything aches."

"I'll make you that coffee." Slowly, each movement an effort as she tried not to shake, she switched the kettle on to boil it again.

"Sorry," Sebastian said. "It's a lot to take in."

Sasha barked. The doorbell sounded.

Sebastian sighed. "I'll see who it is. Probably Daniel. I'd like to talk to him alone, if you don't mind."

"It isn't his fault," she said. "He'll be devastated."

"I know." Sebastian arranged his subdued features into the semblance of a smile. "Why don't you take Sasha for a walk? It's around that time and the dog is stir-crazy."

Lucy waited until he'd started walking upstairs before slipping into his study. The diaries were spread over his desk, a dirty coffee cup next to them. She rifled through the pile while the dog circled the room, barking.

"Hold on, Sasha," Lucy said. "Give me one minute."

The dog took no notice. She either couldn't appreciate the finer points of the English language or chose to ignore them.

Lucy heard Sebastian open the front door and say, "Good morning, officer. How can I help?"

A voice she recognised as Neil Slater's said, in stiff and formal tones, "We have a warrant to search this address."

Lucy's eyes lit on the cream book with pink butterflies. Trembling, she stuffed it into her pocket. "We're going out now, Sasha," she whispered.

Back in the kitchen, she unlocked the French windows with the minimum of noise. Then, hooking a lead onto Sasha's collar, she picked up keys and tiptoed out onto the lawn.

Coatless, Lucy shivered in the chilly garden. It was the least of her problems. "I just need five minutes to read it, Sasha," she said, as she took the dog through the garage and out onto Jackson Road.

CHAPTER 27

LUCY

Jackson Road, busy with traffic, was at least free of police cars. A damp breeze, not quite mist or drizzle, teased at Lucy's body. Adrenaline protected her from the chill. She stopped only when her phone buzzed in her pocket. Thinking it might be a message from Daniel, she was disappointed to see a text from Xander asking if she was okay. She replied, "Tied up. Mum ill", a true statement which omitted almost every relevant detail. How would he react if he discovered she was a murder suspect?

She noticed that she'd missed a call from Daniel too. When she tried to ring back, an error message claimed the network was busy. Mobile reception in Clifton left much to be desired, no doubt because the residents opposed unsightly phone masts. Lucy texted him, "Walking dog. Speak later".

She had no time to waste and didn't remove Sasha's lead to let the dog meander around Christchurch Green. The Samoyed trotted briskly past a line of benches. Lucy had considered sitting there, but the area was too busy for poring over private documents. Locals constantly ambled along the green's criss-cross paths, carrying shopping or walking their own dogs.

A couple of passers-by waved. Sasha attracted an audience as usual, just when Lucy wanted peace and quiet, a place to read without interruption. The Zig Zag would give her that. It was a steep climb, not for the faint-hearted walker, and thus frequently deserted.

She needed to run. Once, Lucy had struggled to match Sasha's pace, but now she tried to coax the dog to move faster. Her mind was racing, too. She'd missed something. If only she could work it out. The more she remembered Jason, the more she was convinced she couldn't have killed him. She'd loved him.

Had it really been love? At thirteen, with hormones swilling around and an attractive man treating her like a human being, she'd thought so.

Sasha barked, cutting into Lucy's awareness. A young mother and toddler stood ahead of them on the path. The little boy held out a biscuit to show the dog.

"Silly child."

Startled by the mother's words, Lucy let the lead slip from her fingers. Suddenly, a memory had surfaced at last. Inside her head, she looked at the dark place where she'd last seen Jason.

She was almost fainting with hunger, but living on celery sticks for a week had been worth it. Her short dress, purchased in the local charity shop, hung loose around her waist. Straightened, lightened locks swung around a face that was surely thinner than a week ago. She looked good.

One hand carried a torch while she used the other to steady herself. The tunnel to the garden cellar had an uneven floor and was tricky to navigate. The light ahead grew brighter. She heard guitar chords as, finally, she stumbled into the vault.

Jason sat alone in the huge arched space. "Hello, Lucy. You're even more beautiful than usual." He stopped strumming and set down the instrument.

She blushed. "What are you working on today?"

"It's a song called 'Lucy is my lover'. How about you? What's new in Lucyland?" His sparkling eyes swept over her.

"We made carrot cake at school. I brought you some."

"In that backpack, is it? You know the way to a man's heart."

Lucy unpacked the cake, a knife, plate and napkins. The scent of cinnamon enveloped her. She ignored her stomach pangs and handed over the sweet food.

Jason cut himself a slice and began to eat. The creamy icing gave him a white moustache, an odd contrast to his dark skin. "Delicious. Aren't you having some?"

"I'm not hungry," she lied.

"Well, I've got a gift for you in exchange. Close your eyes."

She shut them tightly, hearing the steady, slow drip of water from a stalactite as she waited in anticipation. The other girls at school had been boasting about boyfriends, comparing kissers. Would Jason kiss her at last?

"Surprise!" he said.

Feeling a weight in her hand, she flicked her eyelids open. "Oh. A Raymond E Feist book. Thank you. I adore high fantasy."

"Tell me about it. Haven't we spent hours discussing Tolkien? 'Magician' is Feist's best, in my opinion. I've read it over and over."

Lucy started to look inside, noticing the inscription. "Sarah gave this to you?"

"Yes. Can we not talk about her, please? I'd rather focus on my music, this cake and the lovely lady who baked it."

She grinned. "You like my new haircut?"

"Of course."

"Wow. I'm so glad." She smiled, then puckered her lips and moved closer to him, ready to receive a kiss. "I love you, Jason."

"No way." He nearly spat out a mouthful of cake. "Silly child. You can't be serious."

Lucy blinked at him as he shrank from her, his expression shocked and icy. Then she turned and fled.

"Can't you control that dog?" The woman's voice intruded on Lucy's thoughts.

"Pardon?" Lucy stared at the young mother, the wailing toddler and the dog. Sasha skipped around the green, lead trailing after her.

"Your dog stole William's biscuit," the woman accused.

"I'm so sorry." Lucy retrieved Sasha's lead. "Bad dog."

"The council could fine you."

"It won't happen again. Sorry." Heat rose in Lucy's cheeks. She dragged Sasha away from the pair, not daring to look back.

Jason's words still stung. He'd been right, seeing her infatuation for the fantasy it was. Lucy suspected he'd intended to scare her off. If so, he'd succeeded. She'd rushed for her father's whisky bottle. It hadn't made her aggressive, though. Nothing could. She wasn't a confrontational person.

Jennifer, on the other hand, made no secret of it when she disliked someone. She had reserved a particular disdain for Jason, a mixed race dropout. In her view, he was a bad influence on her precious son. It wouldn't have taken much to start a fight with her, especially in those febrile days, when Sarah had left Jason for Daniel. The atmosphere between them was like dry tinder waiting for a spark. Lucy felt like that now, bathed in tension, as if a storm would break and sweep away everything she loved.

"Hello, Lucy."

The voice came from behind as Lucy approached the far side of Christchurch Green. She jolted to a halt, almost dropping the lead again.

"Hi, Brian." She tried not to sound irritated as he overtook her.

Brian's Adidas casuals and trainers suggested a real jogger. He glanced at Lucy's thin velour outfit. "Aren't you cold?"

"I would be if Sasha didn't insist on going so fast."

Brian laughed. "Yes, I wondered who was taking who for a walk."

Why couldn't he leave her alone, just for once? Lucy chided herself at the thought. Unlike haughty Zara, Brian and Marilyn never appeared to judge her. "We're off to the Zig Zag," she said, confident he must be heading elsewhere. The path would be too slippery for runners today.

"I'm going that way myself—"

She gaped at him in dismay.

"—to the Avon Gorge Hotel. A good friend of ours is staying there, and we're planning a run across the Suspension Bridge and out to Ashton Court. You're welcome to come with us if you want to blow away the cobwebs."

"Thank you, but that distance—"

"—is a bridge too far?" Brian interjected. "No worries. Let's canter down to the hotel together."

He left her at the top of the Zig Zag. As she'd expected, it was deserted. Lucy shivered at the rustle of wind through the trees. They were leafless but not bare, covered with the ivy that trailed down the gorge. She fancied she heard Jason's ghost whisper, "Soon you'll know."

She unleashed the dog. Sasha ran down the winding path, little heeding its slipperiness, while Lucy followed as best she could. The crude bench loomed ahead of them.

Lucy skidded to a halt. "Stop."

Sasha obeyed, turning to regard her with an intelligent eye.

"We'll stay here for five minutes," she told the animal.

The bench was damp, wetness soaking through Lucy's velour joggers when she sat down. With a huff, the Samoyed snuggled at her feet, warming them. She noticed she was still wearing slippers.

Placing the dog's lead beside her on the bench, she flexed her stiff fingers. Then she retrieved the butterfly-patterned diary from her pocket. Trembling, she opened it.

The entry for the second of October 2000 began: 'D is in trouble.'

Lucy almost fell backwards, jerking the lead. Sasha stood up, eyes enquiring.

"Sorry." Lucy pushed the dog down to a sitting position. The animal settled peaceably, leaving Lucy to stare at Jennifer's neat, rounded writing.

'He'd argued with Jason. J took advantage of L, got her drunk. When D had words, J attacked him. D picked up carving knife. Stabbed J in self-defence. J dead.'

Moisture blurred Lucy's vision. She felt sick, her stomach heavy. Her brother had killed the man of her dreams and lied about it. Far from using her, Jason had been a gentleman to the last. If Daniel had deceived Jennifer on that score, what further falsehoods had he spread?

A tear splashed onto the page. She realised she'd been carrying a tiny grain of hope that the police were wrong and Jason was still alive. Overwhelmed by grief, she wept for Daniel as well as Jason. The brother she'd always loved and trusted wasn't the person she'd thought. He'd lied to their mother, and he'd tried to persuade Lucy she was to blame. Why would he do that?

The wind whispered to her, "To save his skin, stupid. Because he loves himself, not you."

Lucy sniffed, drying her eyes with her sleeve. She returned her gaze to the journal.

'D waiting for me when I returned from network evening. D desperate, nowhere else to turn. He won't call police. Begged me not to. How can I? He's sure he'd go to jail if I did. Says nobody will believe him. Everyone knows S seduced him and J found out.

Told D I'd help, but saw J in kitchen and had to throw up. Blood everywhere. Told D to get bleach out and clean up his mess. Had large G&T to calm nerves. Then helped D carry J to the old cellar. Told D to make it impassable. D can knock bricks out of walls and ceiling. We'll say it's unstable.' Perhaps Daniel had destroyed too much, ultimately causing the cellar to collapse twenty years later.

Lucy read on. 'In the morning, D will strip J, find J's passport and personal belongings. Everything. J brought it all, because they were going off in Mini tomorrow. Urged D not to be squeamish.'

Lucy turned the page.

'We agreed we must go to France together. I can pass for J if I wear his hat. We'll get across Channel, then we'll pretend J did a Reggie Perrin.'

Lucy had no idea what that meant. She flicked through the next few pages, aware time was running out. When the police searched the house, Sebastian would discover the diary's absence. He would tell them. Sebastian lied when it suited him, but he was oblivious to Jennifer's part in the murder, or so it seemed. If he knew, he'd probably inform them anyway. He was furious and upset with his wife. His loyalties wouldn't necessarily rest with Daniel either.

After formulating their plan, Daniel and his mother had carried it out to the letter. Jennifer had dressed in Jason's clothes. They were about the same size. He was short for a man and she was tall for a woman. The trilby had completed her disguise so successfully that she'd been asked for an autograph, which she provided with aplomb.

Still impersonating Jason, Jennifer had disappeared into the French dunes with his rucksack, finding a quiet spot to change into her own clothes. Jason's garments were left on the beach, along with other items which would identify him. She took the rucksack to Paris on the train, then the Eurostar back to England. Naturally, she'd brought her own passport on the trip.

For two decades, no-one was any the wiser.

Her father was wrong, Lucy reflected. Jennifer didn't just care about herself: she had risked her freedom for her son. Would she have done the same for Lucy?

The dog wriggled, stood up and growled.

"Sasha? What's wrong?" For a crazy moment, Lucy wondered if the dog had absorbed her own anger. Samoyeds were gentle souls, and Lucy had never known Sasha display a hint of aggression.

"Boo!" Daniel's voice sounded behind her. She felt his hand on her shoulder.

Lucy flinched, swivelling to see him leaning against a tree. "You didn't need to creep up on me."

"No, but I enjoyed making you jump." Sunglasses covered his eyes but his grin betrayed amusement. He eased his way round to the front of the bench.

She shrank back, lowering her gaze. "Why did you come here?"

"I spotted you on Jackson Road." His tone was conversational. "There are cops in the crescent, aren't there? I saw their car. I'm surprised Dad called them before talking to me. Anyway, you've got Mum's diary. Well done for giving the police the slip."

She clutched the journal in one hand, holding the dog's collar with the other. "We should talk to the police, Daniel. Tell them."

"Why would I do that?"

"Because they think I did it. Or Mum. I was scared one of us would end up in jail. Either way, she'd have nobody to look after her." Despite her fear, a surge of anger took hold. It surprised her with its intensity, as Sebastian's rage had shocked her earlier. "I can't believe you told Mum it was all about me and Jason."

He shrugged. "I had to get her onside. Anyway, you hero-worshipped him."

Another long-buried memory unfolded. "When I asked you if he'd be interested, you told me to talk to him. Why?"

"These things are best out in the open, aren't they? I thought so, anyway."

"I was only thirteen," she said, with revulsion. "Didn't you think of warning me it was inappropriate?"

"You seemed to know what you wanted." He smirked.

Had he decided to light the touch paper and let it burn for his own entertainment? She stared at him, horrified.

The dog growled again, a warning sign. Daniel might be sunny and charming on the surface, but darkness lurked beneath. Lucy understood that now, and Daniel would know she knew. It would be obvious to him that she'd read Jennifer's account of Jason's death.

"So what did Mum write, then?" he asked.

"Enough. It was all a horrible, sad accident." Grasping how he'd lied and played with her, she wasn't sure. She couldn't afford to let him see that, though. "It's not an easy situation for you, Daniel. I get it. But Mum believed you when you said it was self-defence, so surely the police will."

"Do you believe it was?"

"Of—"

He interrupted. She had hesitated for too long, and he'd noticed.

"There's the problem." Daniel's brow twitched, as if trying to furrow but finding itself paralysed. "If you don't believe me, why should the police? Why would a jury, come to that? Actually, it was self-defence. I didn't want to kill Jason; I wanted him to stay in the band. That's why I prised Sarah away from him. I had to stamp out their little side-hustle. As it happened, Jason and I did argue over you."

"Over me?" Lucy's voice shook.

"I don't know what you'd said to Jason. I heard you stomp upstairs, and I found him in the kitchen. He accused me of pimping you. Then he took a swing at me."

"With a knife?"

"No. But I took one out of the block that Mum kept by the sink. Remember it?"

"Not really." She hadn't paid too much attention to utensils when she wasn't in charge of the kitchen. "But why…?"

"Just to threaten him. He attempted to grab it from me, though, and I stabbed him in the struggle."

"I wish you'd owned up to it then. The police could have done all their forensic tests and proved your story." She tried to sound convincing.

"Don't be silly," Daniel sneered. "My career would have been over. The truth is, once they start asking me questions about Jason, it won't be long before they ask about Gaz. And Brett. And that wasn't self-defence."

She gawped at him. "You mean Jeff deliberately killed Brett?" She paused. "No. You did it. Did you even take him to hospital?"

"Do you need to ask?"

"Gaz? He took a heroin overdose." She recalled the news bulletins and her classmates' taunts about her brother doing drugs. He'd never wanted to discuss it on his rare visits to Bristol.

"Where do you think he got the gear?" Daniel asked. "It was super-pure. He wasn't used to that. I gave him a one-way ticket to the grave."

The dog began to bark and nip at his legs. He frowned.

"Stop that, Sasha!" Lucy tugged the Samoyed's collar, pulling the dog back from her brother. She dare not antagonise him. Even if he didn't have a knife, they were alone on a steep path with broken railings. "Sorry."

"Yes, control that hound, or it's dead meat." Daniel laughed mirthlessly. "You can't work out why I did it, can you?"

Lucy shook her head. Did she want to know? Unfortunately, she already knew too much. That made her a danger to Daniel and him a danger to her. She looked around, desperately wishing for a jogger or walker to appear. Of course, they wouldn't. She'd chosen the Zig Zag for its solitude.

"I didn't do it for fun," Daniel said. "Not like your goldfish and guinea pig. Gaz got too greedy. He'd stepped up to write all the songs, and he wanted all the royalties. That's not how Dr Sweet operated. We were supposed to share."

She froze. "You killed him for that? To get a bigger slice?"

"I got the lot. Pete had left by then, remember. No-one could prove I hadn't written those tunes myself."

"And Brett?"

Daniel spat out, "He turned up, out of the blue, claiming to be my dad. That jackass, Jeff, let him in—"

He quaked with anger, seeming more of a stranger as each second passed. Lucy was silent.

"—so I told Jeff he was on a final warning. He was supposed to keep crazies away, not lay out the welcome mat."

Lucy stared at his hairline and the curve of his cheek, seeing Brett's ghost in his features. His temper would veer off the scale if he knew about Jennifer's other journal. She stayed quiet.

340

"I had a man-to-man chat with Mr Hollande. Or Mr Smith as I understand he's called. He gave me a tall tale about an affair with Mum and how delightful it was to meet his long-lost son at last. You can see what's coming next, can't you?"

"Yes." Lucy suspected Brett had hoped to remind Jennifer about old times and extract cash from her one way or another. He must have been annoyed to find her incapacitated.

"I know a psychopath when I see one," Daniel observed. "After those pleasantries, Brett explained he was stony broke, and he'd be forced to sell his story to the papers soon. You know, to meet his living expenses. Then he said, if I could just help him out with fifty thousand pounds—"

Lucy gasped. "That's a fortune."

"I could afford it, and he knew it." Contempt flashed across Daniel's face. "But I divined that he'd be back again and again. That's how blackmailers work. Maybe I could have got Jeff to rough him up, but why take risks? There was a paper knife to hand, and I used it."

Jeff had been a witness, nothing more. Small wonder he had run from the scene.

Her brother, this stranger, smiled as if confessing the crimes had lightened his burden.

His hand darted forward, snatching the diary from her grasp.

Jumping to her feet, she released her hold on the dog. Her legs wobbled as she tried to grab the book.

Her brother sprang backwards, holding it high in the air, just out of reach. He laughed. There was a hysterical edge to the sound.

"Give it back, Daniel. Please." Her voice quavered. "It proves we're both innocent."

"I don't think so." Daniel shoved her away from him.

She collided with the hard edge of the bench, sending pain shooting through her legs.

Sasha barked, harrying him. He bashed the dog's nose with the diary. The animal whimpered and shied away.

"Leave the dog alone." Lucy staggered towards her brother, making another unsuccessful attempt to clutch the journal.

"I've got to go, sis, and so have you. Thanks for the diary." Daniel thrust the book in his coat pocket. The corner stuck out at a jaunty angle, like a fancy handkerchief. Before she could react, he seized her arms and bundled her around the bench, down the steep slope.

There was no time even to scream. Gravity sent Lucy tumbling, the rocky ground delivering blows and scratches as she bounced downwards. She clawed at a nearby tree, gaining a hold. With her other hand, she clutched at the strands of ivy that smothered the cliff. Luckily, the creeping plant bore her weight. Panting heavily, she controlled her descent, aiming for the foot of the slope where it met a lower branch of the path.

Above her, Daniel stood still, watching her. The smirk played on his lips again. She remembered that amused expression well. He had worn it throughout her childhood, whenever she'd done something cute or funny. Was that all she'd ever been to him: a living toy?

She told herself to keep going. Although bruised and scraped, she didn't appear to have cracked any bones. Once she reached the path, she could run down to the Portway, flag down traffic and seek help.

The Samoyed had recovered from the shock of being attacked and was growling at Daniel again. With a loud curse, he kicked the dog down the hill. Sasha landed on Lucy's head and arms. Dazed, a headache driving into her skull again, Lucy lost her grip.

She fell with the frantic animal onto the path below, hitting the hard surface with a crunch. Agony spiked through her left leg. She groaned, trying to sit up and finding she couldn't. Sasha, seemingly unscathed, scrambled over her body and licked her face.

"How touching. The faithful hound." Daniel towered above her. He must have sprinted round.

She couldn't fight him in her enfeebled state. Lucy closed her eyes. Her best bet was to play dead.

"Enough." Daniel hooked his fingers around the neckline of her top, dragging her roughly along the path.

Limbs, back, shoulders and hips bumped and scraped on the tarmac. Her body shrieked in wordless protest. Lucy bit her lip, not daring even to moan. They were moving uphill. Why? Cautiously, she risked opening her lids a fraction, just enough to peep. Daniel was taking her to a spot where the railings had twisted to one side, revealing an even steeper and longer drop than the one she'd just negotiated. The lethal rock face loomed before her.

Pretending to be dead had been the worst mistake of her life. She was only helping Daniel make it a reality.

She screamed and began to resist, lashing out at his arms and legs. Few punches landed on target. Poor Sasha, nipping at Daniel's heels, received a smack from her. The dog yipped in alarm.

"You're boring me." Daniel yawned. Heedless of the blows rained upon him, he let go of Lucy's garment and shoved her body over the edge, head-first.

There was a mere moment of freefall. Frantically, Lucy flailed out, hands reaching up towards what remained of the railing. She caught hold of Daniel's ankle instead.

If she could just cling onto her brother's leg, perhaps a passer-by would rescue her. Lucy's rational brain told her the chances were slim. So few walkers used the Zig Zag. Yet it was her only hope. She swung her other hand round, so both gripped him, hanging on despite the volley of karate chops to her arms.

Through the pain and fear, she was aware of a kerfuffle, the dog barking and Daniel screaming. Perhaps the animal had bitten him. Suddenly, she was weightless, tumbling through the air with

345

Daniel and Sasha in a flurry of fists, teeth and paws. It was over.

CHAPTER 28

NEIL

"We'll start at the bottom and work up," Neil said. "Can you show me the door to your cellar, please?"

"Follow me," Sebastian said, adding as he led them downstairs to the basement, "It's locked of course."

At the foot of the stairs, a chilly draught assailed them. Sebastian ignored it. "That one." He pointed to a panelled door.

"May I have the key, please?" Neil asked.

"Sorry, I have no idea where it is. We don't use the cellar, as I believe I mentioned."

Sherry smiled at Sebastian. "If you had to guess, where would you start looking for it?"

"In my study, I suppose," the professor admitted.

"Well, that's on this basement level, isn't it? Why don't we start there?" Sherry suggested. "We'll need you to stay with us and supervise the search. I assume that isn't a problem?"

"Not at all." Sebastian visibly stifled a yawn. He seemed more subdued than before.

"Let's begin with your desk," Sherry said. "Oh, what are these?"

Dozens of notebooks lay scattered beside Sebastian's wedding picture. In a variety of bright colours and designs, they looked out of place among his sombre philosophy tomes.

Sebastian paled. "My wife's journals."

Sherry picked one up and opened it. She passed it to Neil. "Recognise the handwriting?"

The rounded letters leaped off the page at him. "The signature on the photos?"

"Could be." She turned to Sebastian. "You say these are Jennifer's? We'll need to take at least one away for analysis. Can you show me her diary for October 2000, please?"

"It should be here. There's a book for every year." He began to sort through them. "How odd. I can't find it."

"We'll look too," Sherry said. "Neil, you put the later years into order and I'll start with the earlier ones, okay?"

When they'd finished the task, it was still missing.

"I'm sure I had the full set when I started reading them last night," Sebastian said. "Maybe

Lucy took it. We can ask her when she returns with the dog."

Neil stiffened. There was no 'maybe' as far as he was concerned. "Where has she gone?" he asked sharply.

"To the Zig Zag, I suppose. Lucy always takes the dog there at 10am. It's her routine." Sebastian shivered. "I don't think she's shut the French windows properly. Mind if we check the kitchen? I'll make you coffee."

"The Zig Zag is a path down the Avon Gorge," Sherry helpfully supplied. "Near the Clifton Suspension Bridge."

"I know where it is." Neil was aware he sounded cross. He'd lived in Bristol for six years, though, and had patronised a fine beer garden overlooking the Zig Zag. Wincing, he imagined Lucy Freeman taking a detour onto the bridge and throwing the journal into the river.

If only he'd known Jennifer Freeman kept diaries. If only he'd asked. Pete Willoughby had pointed the finger at her. Dr Sweet's drummer had been certain Jennifer would have answers, and had even hinted she was a murderess. Now Neil was certain Lucy had run off with valuable evidence, and equally sure that it demonstrated her own guilt. Why would she hide it otherwise?

Neil followed Sebastian and Sherry into the kitchen, finding the French windows wedged open. Sebastian closed them, tutting.

"I'll call Ab. See if he can get the helicopter out," Sherry offered. "How quickly can you get over to the Zig Zag, Neil? I'd suggest you drive."

"Two minutes." He could have strolled there in ten and sprinted in five, but Sherry was right. Time was of the essence and his car was parked nearby.

"Be gentle." Sherry touched Neil's arm, "We don't know enough about Lucy's mental state."

Sebastian stared at her. "You think she might harm herself? We had a nasty shock when we opened my wife's diaries, but I fail to see why Lucy would feel it was her fault."

The air pressure seemed to drop, like the eerie stillness before a downpour. "What did you find out?" Neil asked.

Sebastian's affable demeanour turned frosty. "Private family matters. Nothing relevant to your investigation. My daughter's had mental health issues in the past, but there's no reason why they'd recur now."

"Perhaps because she thinks she could be arrested?" Sherry said softly.

The colour drained from Sebastian's face. "You suspect Lucy of murder? Are you mad? If you've sent her diving off that bridge with your insinuations, you're no better than murderers yourselves." He made for the French windows. "Come on, let's go after her. We've no time to lose."

"Sebastian," Sherry emoted sympathy, "Please stay here. It's for the best. We'll find her as quickly as we can. I'm getting back-up."

Neil flashed Sherry an imploring glance.

"And I'll stay here with you, Sebastian," she said.

Despite the time pressure, Neil took a short detour. Parking by the Suspension Bridge gatehouse, he quizzed the CCTV operator on duty there. The man was used to being asked about potential suicides. To their mutual relief, he told Neil he hadn't seen a woman acting suspiciously, nor had he noticed a white dog. There had been a disturbance on the Zig Zag, though. A pair of joggers had spotted something.

"You just missed them," he said.

Neil thanked him. He spent a further ten seconds standing on the bridge to scan the Avon Gorge. A burst of nostalgia swept over him at the sight of the beer garden. Far below, the river was at low tide, reduced to a still trickle through the mud. Next to it, toy-sized cars flowed freely along the busy Portway. The Zig Zag snaggled down the rocky side of the gorge, mostly obscured by trees. Neil prided himself on 20:20 vision, but he still couldn't spy anything of note. He returned to his car.

It took only a minute to drive to the Avon Gorge Hotel and park by the top of the Zig Zag. Annoyingly, the wiggly path was damp. Neil's smart loafers would slip if he walked too fast on the slick surface. He moved as briskly as was prudent.

The path not only zigged and zagged at odd angles, but it had a camber, as if the builders had merely cut a thin slice out of the rock face. Making it flat was obviously too much effort. Neil thought you could find yourself questioning which way was up. He trod the wet tarmac carefully, hearing and seeing nothing until he reached a bench positioned to offer a view of the Suspension Bridge. Greenery and soil had been disturbed here.

As he scanned the vicinity, a dog's bark cut through the hum of traffic from the Portway.

The sound came from a spot further down. Neil crept as noiselessly as he could. The dog would detect him for sure, but he might yet surprise its human companion.

There was no helicopter yet. Adrenaline coursed through him. He had his chance now. If he found Lucy in time, he'd secure the evidence, arrest her, and solve the murder.

The dog's bark grew louder. Then Neil saw it: the fluffy winter wolf, paws clinging precariously to a patch of ivy twenty feet below. The drop was almost perpendicular, with trees sticking out in odd directions. A fair-haired woman lay straggled across the base of a birch, one arm and leg on each side, as if hugging it. She wore a thin blue leisure suit, quite unsuitable for a cold winter's day.

The dog caught his eye. It barked again, then started licking blood off the woman's hand.

Neil phoned for back-up, to be told it was already on the way, as were the ambulance and fire services. Sherry's foresight impressed him. They'd definitely need the Fire Brigade's ladders. At this point, the path veered off to the right, towards steps that led to the road and away from

Lucy. She was sprawling halfway down a cliff and only vegetation had stopped her plummeting into traffic.

She looked to be in a bad state. Under the dog's steady gaze, using tree roots and clumps of ivy to steady himself, Neil slid down the slope to sit alongside her. His suit trousers wouldn't survive, but Lucy's welfare was more important, even if she was a killer.

If he'd had any doubts, he recognised Lucy as soon as he neared her. Pushing the dog's muzzle away from her hand, he felt her pulse. It was strong and her breathing was regular. Still, she was out for the count. She could be concussed, in shock, or have broken bones. Neil eased his coat off and placed it around her shoulders.

The dog whimpered. A man's voice yelled, "There they are."

Neil flicked his gaze upwards. A uniformed policeman thundered down the path with two middle-aged men dressed in running gear. Neil recognised one of them as Brian Parton.

"She's alive," Neil shouted.

"What about him?" Brian pointed past the birch tree, to a rocky outcrop below. A dark-haired man lay, unmoving, upon it.

CHAPTER 29

LUCY

A bright light filled Lucy's eyes. She blinked.

"Lucy." It was a man's voice. He sounded kind.

She'd heard of near-death experiences when people saw white light, angels and fluffy clouds. Was this an angel, or even God Himself? She'd been taught about Him at school, repeatedly, but hadn't believed in Him until now. She probably shouldn't mention that, not even to blame her father. Sebastian, a determined agnostic, had insisted his children were brought up the same. If they chose to follow a different path as adults, it was up to them. She'd been an adult for fourteen years, though, and God would have expected her to choose by now, wouldn't he?

Pain surged through her, and she cried out. Every single part of her body seemed to hurt, but her left leg was special. It felt as if a bomb had smashed it apart.

"She's coming round," the man said. "Lucy, can you hear me?"

"Yes," she whispered.

The light dimmed. She saw his face peering at her: young, brown-bearded and concerned.

"We're going to take you to hospital, Lucy, and check you over. I've got an ambulance up there waiting, by the hotel. Can you tell me how you're feeling?"

"My leg…" She shivered, suddenly weaker and colder than she had ever been in her life. "Where am I? What happened?"

"You fell down the Avon Gorge, my lover," he said. "Your leg's hurting, is it? You may have fractured it. Can you wiggle your fingers and toes for me, please?"

Lucy obliged. She could feel them, which was encouraging.

"Good girl. We need to assess you properly before giving you painkillers, I'm afraid. How's your head? You've got a lump the size of an egg on your forehead."

He had a strong Bristol accent. It heartened her that she noticed it. She was alive. A spike of elation briefly dampened the pain.

"Headache," she managed to say.

He nodded. "I'm not surprised, my lover. Stay still and quiet, and we'll get you away from here."

Lucy became aware of a warm cushion beside her head. It wriggled, and gave her cheek a surreptitious lick.

356

"Can someone move that dog, please?" her new friend demanded. "You, Neil. Can you stop it licking my patient?"

Through a babble of voices, a man who sounded like Brian volunteered. Lucy saw that it was indeed her neighbour. She was lying on the path by the railings, a group of people around her. Despite her agony, she chuckled to herself. She couldn't imagine Neil Slater taking orders with good grace.

Her mirth was short-lived. Neil loomed above her, officious as ever in his smart suit. It was covered in mud and his shoes were worse. He'd have to clean them, she thought waspishly.

"Lucy Freeman," Neil said. "Remember me? Detective Constable Neil Slater of Avon and Somerset Police. You are under arrest for the murder—"

"Hold on," interrupted the paramedic, less affable now. "You can't do that. This is my patient, and I'm taking her to the BRI."

"Yes, and she could walk out of the hospital and vanish into thin air," Neil retorted. "I'll be coming with you to make sure I get answers in my investigation."

Lucy forced herself to speak. Her head pulsed with pain, and each word added to her torment. "I didn't do it. Daniel killed Jason. It's in Mum's diary."

"The diary that's missing. How convenient." Neil's tone was laced with irony.

She remembered. "Daniel has it."

Her brother had tried to kill her. They had both fallen, but he would have got away, surely? Already, he could have burned the diary to a cinder. Whatever troubles beset ordinary mortals, Daniel, impossibly talented and utterly ruthless, rose above them.

A shudder ran through her, and she gasped in agony. She would be better off in police custody than a hospital, where Daniel could sneak in and finish the job.

"That guy's holding a book." It was another man's voice.

"I see it," Neil said. "I wish they'd get the ladder down to him. He needs medical attention. Unless he's dead and we're looking at another murder charge."

"I told you already," Brian said. "He attacked her, not the other way round. We saw it from the bridge, didn't we, Graham?"

"He was the aggressor, no doubt about it."

"I'll take statements from you both later," Neil said.

"Is that your brother, Lucy?" Brian asked. "Hang on, he's moving. He's ripping the sheets out of that book. Weird."

"No. You have to stop him. Please." Lucy's words emerged as a series of groans. Pain shot through her. She imagined the only proof of her innocence, the pages of Jennifer's diary, floating down the gorge like butterflies.

"We can't reach him." Neil's frustration was palpable.

"He's finished now," Brian said. "Oh no. He's too weak to cling on to the rock. He's falling."

The paramedic gasped. "He jumped."

"A fifty foot drop onto the A4," Brian's friend said.

The ever-present hum of traffic changed its timbre. Metal screeched and clanged. She knew what had happened. It was written in the shocked eyes of the men surrounding her.

Brian's voice was bleak. "I'm sorry, Lucy. There was nothing we could do."

Lucy felt him squeeze her hand. She burst into tears.

CHAPTER 30

NEIL

"You shouldn't have, Neil. How did you know it was my birthday?" Ted Carter eyed the Guilbert's Chocolates bag in Neil's hand.

"You were born on the same day as my girlfriend, sir. What are the odds of that?"

"I suspect I arrived in this world a few years before her." Ted winked. "She's down in south Somerset, isn't she? If you're travelling out to the M5, I can recommend the flowers at Gordano services. A bunch of lilies always goes down well with the ladies."

"Thanks for the tip." He knew Gemma well enough to ignore it. She had views on sustainability. Their relationship wouldn't last five minutes if he bought her blooms flown in from faraway lands. He had done well to find chocolates made in Bristol. Of course, Sherry had stepped in to help. It did no harm to consult an expert.

"Well done on Op Indigo, by the way. Ab mentioned you'd had a hunch about the Freeman family all along."

Neil nodded. Ab had been generous. A Freeman was responsible for Jason Jardine's death, but it wasn't the person Neil expected.

"We've had CCTV reports back from the Met and Surrey Police," Ted continued. "As you'd suppose, there weren't any cameras in the country lane where Brett Smith's body was dumped. But Dan Freeman's car was traced nearby at around the estimated time of death."

"Which backs up Lucy Freeman's account, sir."

"Exactly. As well as other evidence. I'm expecting mobile phone records soon. Well, I'd better dash. Enjoy your weekend."

"You too."

Neil mulled over Ted's words as he joined the Friday night rush hour traffic heading out of Bristol. Lucy Freeman had lied to them, probably more than once. That didn't make her guilty, though. People told falsehoods for a variety of reasons. It would serve him well to remember that.

Once he'd listened to her, really listened, and they'd checked out her story, pieces had fallen into place like a jigsaw. Sebastian had confirmed that the diaries contained his wife's handwriting, and a specialist had matched it with the Dr Sweet photograph on file. Not all of the missing book's pages could be recovered, but enough had survived to explain Jennifer's trip to France. They also had proof that she'd returned on the Eurostar.

It was a shame Dan Freeman hadn't survived to be brought to justice for his crimes. Nor, thanks to her poor health, would Jennifer face a court of law. She hadn't just covered up Jason's death, as it turned out, she'd also known that her daughter had given Neil hash brownies.

It seemed this had been an honest mistake on Lucy's part. One of Dan's friends had left the cakes for him and she didn't know about the added extra.

Coincidentally, Gemma had coffee and brownies waiting for him when he arrived at the B&B. "A special recipe," she told him.

"No secret ingredients, I trust?"

She coloured up. "Maybe. Why not try one?"

He took a bite. "Delicious."

She tapped the side of her nose. "Beetroot and dark chocolate. Lush, aren't they?"

"Wonderful. What would you like to do this evening? I thought we might get vegan burgers at the Riflemans Arms."

"I'd love that." Gemma stared at him. "Yours will be 100% beef, I assume?"

"I'm planning to try the plant-based option."

Her smile was like the warmest sunshine. "What's happened to you? You're more open all of a sudden."

"I hope so." He hugged her.

6 MONTHS LATER

CHAPTER 31

LUCY

Lucy twisted a lock of fair hair around her finger. She hadn't tied it back today. It hung long and loose around the shoulders of her new white cotton T-shirt.

Although she admired the vivid summer dresses of the other patrons, she still preferred to blend into the background. She didn't feel part of Clifton Village's café culture yet. Cups and saucers clattered as they were set down on the outdoor tables. Snatches of conversation drifted through the warm air. She watched and listened, sipping hot chocolate. Sunshine reflected off its glossy surface and intensified the colours all around her. It was as if the world had finally woken from a long sleep.

Trying to make the drink last, she studied the bright young people working or mingling around her. Meeting a boy for coffee was something that should have happened when she was a teenager, but never did. Lucy wasn't even certain she wanted it now. She'd only agreed because Xander kept pressing her. Finally, he eliminated her objections by offering to travel from London to Clifton. He was late, though. Perhaps he'd had second thoughts.

With a start, she noticed Neil, the policeman. He was strolling past the ice-cream-coloured buildings opposite, holding hands with a young woman. Her long black hair swung as she walked. She looked familiar. Lucy couldn't place her and was glad it wasn't Sherry. The policewoman was far too charming to be tied to grumpy Neil outside her work.

Today, he didn't appear so cranky. He smiled at his girlfriend and received a grin in return. It was the kind of day when everyone seemed happy.

The brunette held Lucy's gaze for a second, then turned away and whispered something that sounded like, "Isn't that the girl who gave you drugs?"

"It was a misunderstanding," Lucy heard Neil say, just as she identified his companion. The couple had been together in the city centre arcade where little Freya had a haircut. A tremor of apprehension shook Lucy as she realised they were crossing the road towards her. She had made

her peace with Neil's suspicions about her –
everyone made mistakes, after all – but that didn't
mean she wanted to socialise with him.

The girl's green eyes twinkled. "Hello. We met
before, but we weren't introduced. I'm Gemma,
Neil's fiancée."

"We just got engaged last month." Neil sounded
uneasy. It clearly hadn't been his idea to stop.

"Congratulations," Lucy said. She understood
the rules. You were supposed to say this.

"Want to see my ring?" Without waiting for a
reply, Gemma splayed out the fingers of her left
hand. They were long and elegant, a perfect foil
for the silver band. It had no stone, instead being
etched with an elaborate knotted design.

Lucy gasped. "That's so pretty. Is it Celtic?"

"The Celtic symbol for love." Gemma beamed.

"I'm very pleased for you." Lucy meant it. An
aura of peace surrounded Gemma. The girl plainly
adored Neil, and she smoothed his rough edges.
He stood a chance of becoming a decent human
being.

"Do you live round here?" Gemma asked.

"For now."

"We're in Leigh Woods," Gemma said. "The Somerset side of the Suspension Bridge. So we're almost your neighbours."

"I know it. I walk there sometimes with the dog," Lucy explained. "Not for much longer, though. Our house is up for sale. Dad said there were too many ghosts."

"Only one dead body, surely?" Neil's eyes had that familiar inquisitive look.

Lucy used all her willpower to return his stare without trembling. "There's Daniel as well." That wasn't all, of course. Although she wouldn't voice them to Neil, she understood Sebastian's reasons. Number 13 was haunted by the living: her father's memories of Jennifer, and the woman he thought she'd been. The construct he'd built of his wife was as much a phantom as any skeleton raised from a sinkhole.

Jennifer had taken a turn for the worse. She was receiving end-of-life care in a hospice. Sebastian appeared to be mourning her already. He wanted to move on. Lucy must do so too.

"Where will you go next?" Gemma asked.

"I don't know. I'll rent a flat for a few months, while I decide what to do." She'd stay close to Jennifer until the end. Then there would be grief, but also a new beginning. Lucy would have choices. Perhaps she could pursue a career in music. Away from Bristol, no-one would compare her with Daniel.

It was time for her life to happen. She'd waited long enough.

Just as Lucy had resigned herself to asking if they wanted to share her table, a tall, slightly plump young man ambled around the corner. He wore sneakers, jeans and a black T-shirt emblazoned with an image of Gandalf.

"Xander!" It couldn't be anyone else, but Lucy still felt a surge of relief as he strolled over to her.

"Lucy." He smiled, blue eyes blinking in the sun. "Forgive me, I didn't realise we'd have company."

"These are—" Lucy struggled to find the word, as they weren't her friends, "—acquaintances of mine, Neil and Gemma."

"I'm Xander." The men shook hands.

"Nice to meet you. We were just leaving." Neil stepped off the pavement and into the road.

Gemma stayed for a few moments. "I'm delighted our paths crossed," she said to Xander, her voice earnest. "Look after Lucy, okay? Because she's worth it." With a wink towards

Lucy, she hooked her arm in Neil's and let him lead her away.

Lucy reddened. She realised Xander was blushing too.

"No pressure," he said, sitting down opposite.

Suddenly tongue-tied, she studied him. His hair was fine and white-blond, his features amiable. He didn't look like the armour-suited fighter she knew from the computer screen. Then again, she was not a willowy minstrel in real life.

"I'm sorry I'm late," he said. "Thanks for waiting. I thought the local railway station would be nearby, but it's a mile away. Anyway, the cakes look amazing, so why don't I get us each a slice? What do you recommend?" He paused. "Ah. Have I put my foot in it?"

Lucy chewed her lip. "No. Not anymore. I used to have a problem with my weight."

"I can't imagine that." Xander's gaze swept her body. "You're perfect."

She flushed even more. "I borrowed a dog. We go for walks." While Sasha had moved back in with Margaret, the retired teacher happily handed the leash to Lucy every day. After six months, she was down to a size 12. Cheekbones had emerged too, lending her an uncanny resemblance to a young Jennifer. Lucy wasn't sure she liked that.

Xander obviously did. His eyes were kind: he'd meant the compliment. He couldn't know she wasn't used to them.

"Dogs are awesome," he said. "What sort is it?"

"A Samoyed. She's called Sasha." Her awkwardness started to vanish. On impulse, she offered, "We can take her out later, if you like."

"Very much. But first, cake. You didn't answer my question."

"Anything with chocolate, please."

He went inside. A pang of anxiety churned Lucy's stomach. She quelled it by people-watching. Maybe she would risk some new clothes, or at least new-to-her garments from a charity shop. She could ask Freya's mother for style tips.

It seemed an age before Xander emerged with a tray of drinks and brownies. He sat down and took a huge bite. "These are the best."

"Worth a trip from London?"

"Definitely. And I must admit, I'm relieved to find you really are a girl. After five years of in-game raids, I thought I knew you. But, as the train drew closer to Bristol, I began to wonder if you were a serial killer."

Should she tell him? Lucy made a snap decision. Heart thumping, she took out her phone to show him a news article. "It's funny you should say that, because my brother was. Look."

"He tried to kill you?" Xander's eyes were wide with sympathy. "Lucky for us that he failed."

Lucy's heart leaped a little at the word 'us'. She pushed the thought away, nibbling her brownie. It really was the best ever.

She smiled at Xander. After five years of online friendship, she felt sure he wasn't a serial killer either. Maybe a spark would flare between them. She'd know soon enough. If it didn't, that was all right, too. They'd still be friends.

She wasn't looking for love from Xander, because she'd already found it closer to home.

It was never too late to start loving yourself.

ooo0ooo

He stole her childhood. Can she escape before he takes her life?

BRIGHT LIES is AA Abbott's darkest psychological thriller. Look inside to start reading:

https://mybook.to/BrightLiesLargePrint

ooo0ooo

AA Abbott has also written the **Trail series** of thrillers, a lighter read sizzling with suspense and family drama. Take look at the first book in

the series, **THE BRIDE'S TRAIL. Shady friends and sinister secrets. When a shy graduate finds herself framed, can she survive long enough to clear her name?**

https://mybook.to/TheBridesTrailDyslexia

Visit AA Abbott's website to find out more, and sign up for her newsletter to receive a free ebook of short stories, news and offers.

https://aaabbott.co.uk

ooo0ooo

Did you enjoy **LIES AT HER DOOR?** Help other readers find their next psychological thriller – review this book on Amazon and Goodreads.

Amazon:
https://mybook.to/LiesatHerDoorLargePrnt

https://www.goodreads.com/book/show/61237947-lies-at-her-door

ooo0ooo

ABOUT THE AUTHOR

British author AA Abbott, also known as Helen, writes suspense thrillers about women who find their inner strength when they're facing deadly danger. Like Lucy Freeman, she lives in a tall, thin house in Bristol. She's also lived and worked in London and Birmingham, so all three cities feature in her intelligent and pacy novels.

While Helen is not dyslexic, many of her family are, which is why she is especially keen to make her books accessible. All of them are available in dyslexia-friendly large print as well as standard ebook and paperback editions. BRIGHT LIES is also available as an audiobook, recorded by award-winning voice actor Elidh Beaton.

Find out more on Helen's website
https://aaabbott.co.uk/

Say hello on Facebook

https://www.facebook.com/AAAbbottStories/

Follow on Twitter

https://www.twitter.com/AAAbbottStories

ooo0ooo

BOOKS BY A.A. ABBOTT

Up In Smoke

After The Interview

The Bride's Trail

The Vodka Trail

The Grass Trail

The Revenge Trail

The Final Trail

Bright Lies

Lies at Her Door

All books are available in ebook, standard paperback and large print (super-easy to read). BRIGHT LIES is also available in audiobook.

ooo0ooo

ABOUT BRIGHT LIES, AA ABBOTT'S DARKEST THRILLER

He stole her childhood. Can she escape before he takes her life?

Emily longs to be an artist. Her dream comes true when her new stepfather, a rich painter, begins mentoring her. But she's shocked to discover his dark side, and fear sends her fleeing his fancy home.

After facing further danger in a night on the streets, Emily accepts shelter in a squat. Building a future as an artist, she's terrified to learn her stepfather has turned to the media to hunt her down. Can she survive betrayal by her new friends and escape a killer's revenge?

If you enjoy nail-biting suspense, slow-burning secrets and dark domestic noir, you'll love AA Abbott's chilling psychological thriller.

Read BRIGHT LIES today and stay by Emily's side as she runs for her life!

https://mybook.to/BrightLiesLargePrint

ooo0ooo